THE COST OF LETTERS

The Cost of Letters

A Survey of Literary Living Standards

edited by Andrew Holgate and

Honor Wilson-Fletcher

A W Magazine Publication

First published in Great Britain in 1998
by Waterstone's, Capital Court
Capital Interchange Way
Brentford, Middlesex TW8 0EX

© Waterstone's Booksellers Ltd 1998

Page 209 constitutes an extension of this copyright page

A CIP catalogue record for this book is available from the British
Library

ISBN 0 9527405 9 1

Typeset in New Baskerville by Parker Typesetting, Leicester

Printed and bound in Great Britain by Cox & Wyman Ltd, Reading,
Berkshire

Contents

Foreword

by Andrew Holgate and
Honor Wilson-Fletcher

Money is not something most of us think about when reading a book. It may be something we're resigned to dealing with in our everyday lives; it is not, however, what we want to face when engaged in the solitary, meditative exercise of reading.

And yet, as this survey of literary living standards makes abundantly clear, money – and, often, the lack of it – is intimately bound up with the whole process of writing. Anyone looking in this survey of literary living standards for lurid tales of sky-high advances and lotus-eating lifestyles may get something of a shock when reading the responses of our contributors. Many of the writers who have replied to our questionnaire are very well known and, in literary terms, extremely successful (just count the number of awards); yet even the most 'honoured' of them seem acutely aware of the insecurity of writing as a profession, the huge difficulty of earning a living from it, and the precarious hold authors have on the loyalty and attention of their readers.

With such a poor prospect of financial success, the obvious question, is, why do it? Overwhelmingly, the response from the authors included in this book was that writing was both necessary, and a gift. Our contributors have of course 'made it' – in the sense that they are still writing rather than accounting, gardening or lighthouse-keeping – and we can pass no comment on the plight of those who are forced, for whatever reason, to quit. It is worth bearing this in mind when reading the contributions that follow: the modest expectations of the authors who agreed to contribute are those of some of our most prestigious and respected authors. This book should be required reading for any student of creative writing.

The original idea for this volume came from Alain de Botton, himself a successful novelist and non-fiction writer. He had come across a survey of literary living standards conducted in 1946 by a cash-strapped Cyril Connolly in his literary magazine *Horizon*. Connolly had asked a number of fellow authors six straightforward questions about how much they felt a writer needed to earn, whether this target could be achieved solely by writing, and, if not, what other occupations a writer should consider. He also, very pertinently, asked them whether they felt the State should be helping to alleviate their financial position. Twenty-one authors (including Connolly himself) replied to the questionnaire, and their answers were printed in the September 1946 issue of *Horizon*.

What began as an idea for an article in Waterstone's W magazine – 'Have things changed much for writers since 1946?' – quickly grew, in the white heat of Alain's enthusiasm, into a proposal for a whole book. Gary McKeone, Literature Director at the Arts Council of England, generously agreed to help fund the project, and a long list of contemporary authors was drawn up. That so many of them have replied, and been so candid in their responses, is testament to Alain and Gary, and also to the extraordinary passion the subject stirs up amongst writers.

So why is Waterstone's publishing this collective report? Quite simply to spark debate. *The Cost of Letters* is published at a time of genuine concern about the funding of writing. A few high-profile advances cannot mask the changed nature of the relationship between author and publisher – quite a few authors in the modern survey, for instance, look back wistfully to a time when publishers weren't so governed by the balance sheet and were prepared to spend a good deal of time 'nurturing' talent. Are we offering sufficient support for new writing? Or should we be spending our money encouraging more people to read or support our public libraries more wholeheartedly? Any organisation with a stake in the vitality of writing must be considering questions like these. Britain has a colossal heritage of great writing – it surely cannot hurt to consider how we might ensure a similarly dynamic future. The forty-two contemporary authors included here don't always agree on a way ahead for the funding of literature (in fact, taken by and large, they agree on very little); but they do show, sometimes quite dramatically, how financially hazardous is the plight of the contemporary writer.

Events have also conspired to make this publication unusually timely. The Arts Council itself is looking hard at how it distributes the money it has in its gift, and the holding of a two-day conference in Warwick at the end of May 1998 entitled 'The Needs of Writers: Support for Literature Today and in History' is given added spice by rumours that the government is thinking of holding a similar conference itself in the near future.

A few words of clarification are needed about the terms of reference of this survey. Cyril Connolly addressed his six questions to what he called 'serious' writers. Several contemporary authors have, quite rightly, taken issue with the term, but we felt we had to keep faith with it when the time came to choose our own list of writers. We have tried to cast our net as wide as possible, including poets, biographers and historians as well as novelists, but we have also tried to ensure that respondents would be able to talk specifically about the situation in Britain. (Paul Durcan's reply, however, offers an interesting view from Dublin.)

The authors who replied to the survey in 1998 were asked exactly the same questions as the 1946 respondents (Connolly's habit of referring to a writer only as 'he' did not pass without comment). The original 1946 questionnaire actually drew replies from twenty-one authors, but considerations of space and length have meant that we did not have room for the replies from several contributors – Robert Ironside, John Russell, Edward Sackville-West, William Sansom and D.S. Savage.

There are many people to thank for ensuring the success of this project, but we would like to acknowledge our debt and express our thanks in particular to the following – Alain de Botton, for having a great idea he was kind enough to share with us, and for the generosity he has consistently demonstrated since then; Gary McKeone and the Arts Council, for matching our enthusiasm and giving us financial assistance; all the authors who consented to take part in this project and convinced us it was worthwhile; the agents and estates who gave us permission to reprint excerpts from the 1946 *Horizon* article; and finally, of course, Cyril Connolly himself.

Some notes on the text

Anyone wishing to compare the financial aspirations of writers in 1946 and 1998 should adopt the calculation used by Alain de Botton in his introduction and multiply any 1946 figure by twenty.

The following definitions may also prove useful:

Public Lending Right *A payment made to authors from public funds each year, the amount being proportional to the number of times that the author's book or books have been borrowed during the course of the previous year, to a maximum of £6000.*

Advances and royalties *Book deals generally include an element of both advance and royalty payment. An advance is a payment made prior to publication, and royalties are a percentage of monies made from the sale of the book after any advance has 'earned out'.*

The Royal Literary Fund *Founded in the 1790s to assist writers and their families who face hardship, but not to fund projects.*

The Writers Guild of Great Britain *Affiliated to the TUC, a trade union that represents writers' interests in film, TV, theatre and publishing and discusses up to government-level legislation affecting, for example, copyright.*

The Royal Society of Literature *Holds lectures and debates and tries to foster the best in writing, and is open to any individual with an interest in literature. The Society administers two annual awards for writing and has the responsibility of conferring the title of Companion of Literature on authors considered to be of 'conspicuous attainment in English Literature'.*

The Arvon Foundation *A charity with centres in Devon, Yorkshire and Scotland offering courses to enable students of literature to work alongside professional and established writers.*

The Society of Authors *Established in 1884 as both a limited company and independent trade union offering an increasingly diverse range of legal and general advice to assist and protect authors.*

If you would like to write to us on the subject of the Cost of Letters, please send your correspondence to: Honor Wilson-Fletcher, Waterstone's, Capital Court, Capital Interchange Way, Brentford, Middx TW8 0EX. You can also email us on honor.wilson-fletcher@waterstones.co.uk

Introduction

by Alain de Botton

1. There are few details about someone as intriguing as the size of
their salary. Despite some impressive attempts (Socrates, Jesus) to
persuade us to think otherwise, money is still the most widely-
accepted indicator of a person's standing in the world. In the case of
writers, money is especially fascinating. After all, it isn't so boring
just to learn what writers have for breakfast. Nietzsche loved cheese
omelettes. Henry James ate peaches. But if their cash is of most
interest, it's perhaps because of the unusual fit between money and
art. It seems impossible to measure the value of literary works in
purely financial terms, it makes no sense to ask what *Middlemarch* or
Pride and Prejudice are worth. And yet for George Eliot and Jane
Austen, these works did result in particular sums which were
handed over by booksellers and went to pay for particular things
like marmalade and stockings. Learning how much writers are paid
for their works illuminates the interrelation between the world of
money and the world of art. In looking at writers' account books
and cheque stubs, it seems we glimpse nothing less than a point of
connection between the earthly and spiritual realms.

2. A connection which could in general hardly be more depressing
for writers. Poverty and literature have a shamefully long joint
history. The list of major authors whose lives were blighted by
financial anxieties contradicts any comfortable assumptions of a link
between artistic merit and economic reward, assumptions that great
art must inevitably lead to great fortunes. In part, the difficulty of
making even a modest living from one's pen stems from the

extraordinarily large number of books which an author is obliged to sell. To earn £20,000, an author whose book retails for £10 would – at a typical royalty rate of 10% – have to sell 20,000 copies. Most serious works sell no more than five or six thousand.

Then there is the difficulty of remaining productive over long periods. Few writers are able to turn out a decent book a year, three or four years is more typically necessary, and even this rate is unlikely to go on over an entire working life. The idea of a Muse may be fanciful and sexually incorrect, but the lady evokes well enough the insecurity of the hold most writers have on their creative faculties. An element of chance lurks behind the birth of masterpieces, which aggravates financial anxieties: it is one thing to be poor and convinced of the worth of one's work, far harder to combine poverty with an awareness a book isn't going well.

Writing is unfortunately rather less generous towards mediocrity than other professions. A mediocre solicitor can do useful work, enjoy a comfortable salary and the respect of the community. So may a mediocre hairdresser, radio producer or travel agent. The mediocre writer on the other hand – and few writers can entirely escape the suspicion that they are mediocre – risks both a more self-loathing and a more poverty-stricken fate. Which is not helped by the degree of *schadenfreude* others tend to feel at writers' troubles; it seems enough people aspire to literary works to be rather cheered by the spectacle of writers who have run aground pursuing a goal they may themselves secretly have coveted.

To escape the poverty and attendant anxieties, writers have always had to look outside for help. Until the middle of the eighteenth century, this meant a patron, an aristocrat or prosperous merchant, who would dispense lodgings, dinners, introductions and cash in exchange for flattering dedications. Hobbes, Dryden, Pope, Fielding, Smollett, Gibbon were among the many beneficiaries of the system. But it wasn't perfect. Macaulay judged it led to a degrading 'traffic in praise' and left a writer 'in morals something between a panderer and a beggar'. In a letter to the Earl of Chesterfield (who had refused him help at a vulnerable point in his career), Samuel

Johnson remarked bitterly: 'Is not a patron, My Lord, one who looks with unconcern on a man struggling for life in the water and when he has reached ground encumbers him with help?' The birth of a mass readership towards the end of the eighteenth century signalled the end of the patronage system, which was replaced by the writer's modern reliance on book sales, with additional help from newspapers, and in the twentieth century, advertising, radio, television and academia.

But it has, of course, never been enough.

3. Cyril Connolly (1903-1974) was particularly worried. For the essayist and critic, the relationship between writing and money was a life-long obsession, a theme running through his two most important books, *Enemies of Promise* (1938) and *The Unquiet Grave* (1944), and in his editorship of the literary magazine, *Horizon*. Too fond of travelling, not working and getting divorced, Connolly was permanently on the lookout for ways to generate more cash. In *Enemies of Promise*, he suggested a number of fanciful schemes. My favourite: 'I should like to see a custom introduced of readers who are pleased with a book sending the author some small cash token: anything between half-a-crown and a hundred pounds [£2,000 in 1998]. Authors would then receive what their publishers give them as a flat rate and their "tips" from grateful readers in addition.' Financial anxieties were, according to Connolly, the greatest of all the enemies of promise: 'What ruins young writers is over-production. The need for money is what causes over-production; therefore writers must have private incomes,' which even in 1938 would have sounded flip. But what if, like Connolly himself, writers weren't lucky enough to have been born with a trust fund?

In the summer of 1946, Connolly decided that the subject deserved more thorough consideration, and to this end, he sought to discover what solutions his fellow practitioners had discovered to weather the economic uncertainties of writing. From the offices of *Horizon*, he sent the following questionnaire to a selection of leading British writers.

1. How much do you think a writer needs to live on?

2. Do you think a serious writer can earn this sum by his writing, and if so, how?

3. If not, what do you think is the most suitable second occupation for him?

4. Do you think literature suffers from the diversion of a writer's energy into other employments or is enriched by it?

5. Do you think the State or any other institution should do more for writers?

6. Are you satisfied with your own solution of the problem and have you any specific advice to give young people who wish to earn their living by writing?

Twenty-one writers answered, among them John Betjeman, Elizabeth Bowen, Cecil Day Lewis, Robert Graves, Laurie Lee, George Orwell, V. S. Pritchett, Stephen Spender and Dylan Thomas, and Connolly published their replies in a special issue of *Horizon* (September, 1946), entitled 'The Cost of Letters'.

More than fifty years later, their answers remain fascinating. It is not just that these important writers were disclosing some of their most private thoughts (few things are as private as money), it is also that the issues raised by the questionnaire are still likely to confront anyone writing today. How much money does one need? How can one raise the necessary sum?

Waterstone's was intrigued, as was the Arts Council, and together they arranged to put Connolly's questions to a new generation of writers (we agreed that each writer should receive a book token worth £200 in exchange). So 'The Cost of Letters' was sent out to, among others, Julian Barnes, Sebastian Faulks, Will Self, Beryl Bainbridge, Fay Weldon, Hilary Mantel, Rose Tremain, Michael Holroyd, Victoria Glendinning, Michèle Roberts, A. L. Kennedy, Penelope Lively and Alasdair Gray.

The result will hopefully draw attention to the serious financial problems facing writers and help contribute to future decisions on the funding of literature (by the Arts Council and other bodies). A major survey of how British writers feel about money may also provide, for some at least, a touch of what is coyly known as human interest.

4. What united the writers of today and 1946 was agreement on the enormous difficulties facing anyone trying to earn a living by their pen – though there were some interesting disagreements about how much a writer would actually need to live on. To quote a sample:

Suggested per annum income for writers

1946 (converted into today's currency, £1 in 1946 = £20 today):

Cecil Day Lewis	£6,000
Robert Kee	£8,000
George Orwell	£20,000
Stephen Spender	£20,000
V. S. Pritchett	£24,000
Elizabeth Bowen	£70,000

1998:

Alasdair Gray	£20,000 approx.
Fay Weldon	£26,000
Lucy Ellman	£20,000-£50,000
Alice Thomas Ellis	£30,000
Will Self	£40,000-£80,000 (approx.)
Michael Holroyd	£70,000

Many of today's writers went out of their way to stress that they were not asking for more than anyone else. 'Writers are part of humanity. We don't need special treatment,' said Michèle Roberts. 'Frankly, in a country with no minimum wage and an appalling percentage of the population unable to buy adequate food, the – sometimes self-inflicted – financial gripes of writers wouldn't be my first concern,' argued A. L. Kennedy, which may reassure her publisher.

It was left to a handful of writers to make more ambitious claims; what if wealth was more conducive to literature than the national average wage? 'I suppose there's a remote chance that a prosperous writer might lose touch with the real world,' conceded Lucy Ellmann, though the danger didn't seem acute: 'What really happens to a writer given infinite access to SMOKED SALMON?' Only Hilary Mantel dared to state the obvious, that all published writers should be 'as rich as Croesus. They could then indulge in dissipation and eccentricity on a scale the public has a right to expect . . . To engage the interest of the Sunday papers, it is necessary to build up a big drug habit. Female writers absolutely must not be seen to dress out of Marks & Spencers. Also, writers who venture abroad must always travel first class and stay at the best hotels. Otherwise, they encounter hazards and hardships, write very dull books about them, and become a burden to the spirit.'

5. But if book sales don't stretch far enough to pay for the first-class ticket, what is the best second occupation for a writer? In 1946, John Betjeman suggested the job of station-master on a small country branch line (single track). Cyril Connolly proposed 'a rich wife' (he had married an American heiress). And George Orwell argued that writers should always pursue non-literary employment (he mentioned working in a bank or an insurance firm), rather than 'semi-creative work such as teaching, broadcasting or composing propaganda for bodies such as the British Council'.

The prejudice against 'semi-creative' work has only increased since Orwell's time. Journalism emerged as a particular bugbear of today's writers; many judged almost any other occupation preferable, it was better to work at a supermarket check-out, or as a gardener – a curious line if one considers just how many writers (and many of the ones who themselves attacked journalism) work regularly for newspapers.

It was striking to note just how few of the writers we surveyed in fact have serious second careers – reflected in the playful (or plain frivolous) nature of many of their answers. Despite advice that one might write and, for instance, be a doctor or insurance salesman, few writers are able to do anything besides write – and contribute to newspapers. Much of the problem lies in the difficulty of finding work that complements a writing life. A second occupation may benefit writing, but too often it merely threatens to supplant it completely. Most jobs require hours that make writing impossible; John Stuart Mill would today have a hard time finding anything as congenial as his five mornings a week at the East India Company. Work at the BBC or within academia – once standard options for writers – has become impossibly competitive, and consequently no more secure than writing itself. In this context, one can see why, though it may not be ideal, journalism remains one of the more realistic ways to pay for one's writing.

6. When Cyril Connolly sent out his original questionnaire, a Labour government had just started to create the welfare state, and many writers assumed that it was the government's responsibility – through the Arts Council – to take an active role in funding literature. By contributing to national well-being, glory and happiness, serious literature was no less worthy of public funds than hospitals or schools. The Thatcher-Major years have changed the tone. Indeed many now reject outright the idea of spending state funds on literature ('Who needs writers?' wondered Beryl Bainbridge, a much-needed figure).

Nevertheless, a great many writers argued for some kind of institutional change. Abolishing income tax for writers was one popular idea, borrowed from the enlightened policy of the Irish Republic. And in a spirit imical to New Labour, there were suggestions of co-operation between the public and private sectors, a return to a kind of patronage system, whereby firms could fund writers to complete projects, in exchange for a word of thanks (writing is extremely cheap next to an opera or an exhibition).

Publishers were frequently charged with worsening the financial situation of authors. They were accused of stinginess over royalties and madness in awarding such large advances to certain writers.

Many felt there should be limits set on the size of advances, because they saw a connection between the wealth of a few writers and the poverty of the majority. By restraining the amount that publishers could pay any one writer, more writers would earn decent advances (an example of the theory that many people are poor because a few people are very rich).

7. As for advice to younger writers, those polled were (perhaps predictably) modest: 'I wouldn't presume to advise anyone to write or not write,' said A. L. Kennedy. There was a consensus that writing was not a career, but a vocation ('If you are hell bent on writing you will do it anyway,' said Penelope Lively), and that a beginner would have to be 'content to be poor for quite a long time' (Victoria Glendinning).

But perhaps most significantly, all writers, even the most established ones, agreed that money was a live problem for them. In airing their thoughts on the subject, they will certainly help anyone pursuing a literary career to feel less personally beset by, and less lonely with, their own financial anxieties.

ALAIN DE BOTTON *is the author of three novels* – Essays in Love, The Romantic Movement *and* Kiss and Tell – *and a work of non-fiction,* How Proust Can Change Your Life, *which was published in paperback in March 1998.*

1998

Simon Armitage

1. *How much do you think a writer needs to live on?*

It's impossible to say – there are too many variables such as where a writer lives or the number of dependents (family, bodyguards, etc). Also, writers are so different in their needs. One author might find inspiration living in a broken-down bus at the edge of the wood, eating moss and drinking the morning dew, another might not be able to function without slippers, smoking jacket and the remote-control to hand.

It's probably more useful to talk about personal experience than to generalise, and a couple of years ago I lived in a rented house, on my own, in probably one of the cheapest parts of the country. I reckon I got by on about £500 a month, which is what, £6,000 a year, which is nothing (unless you've got nothing, in which case it's plenty). Having said that, my travelling expenses alone for that year were over £7,000, a lot of which had to be forked out in advance, so I needed some kind of kitty or float to be able to earn. At some points in my life it's suited me to be skint.

2. *Do you think a serious writer can earn this sum by his writing, and if so, how?*

Royalties tend to come to mind when there's talk of earning money from writing, either as money advanced by the publisher or income from book sales. I don't know about novelists – that's another planet – but I'd guess that in Britain and Ireland there are about four or five poets only who make a living wage from that source, two of whom would be categorised as writers of light verse. There might be a few more who travel under the banner of poet in the field of literature but are actually entertainers in the field of show business.

Most poets earn money from engagements connected with writing rather than writing itself, engagements such as readings or teaching, or by having an actual job. Again, speaking personally rather than for everyone, I've always found it useful not to see writing as a career, but to think of it instead as stolen time or a kind of luxury. I'd be suspicious (I am suspicious) of anyone who thought of poetry as a system of salary-points and promotions. Graves recommended that each poem be seen as part of the process of becoming a poet rather than another rung on the ladder of a career in literature, and I think that's a pretty good code of practice. Better as well to think of your own work in terms of progression and improvement rather than success and worth. I wonder if there might be a general rule here; that those who set out to make a particular sum through poetry will probably fail, whereas those who concentrate on their writing might well achieve a living income almost by default or accident. If it isn't true it should be.

3. *If not, what do you think is the most suitable second occupation for him?*

One with time for day-dreaming.

4. *Do you think literature suffers from the diversion of a writer's energy into other employments or is enriched by it?*

Works both ways, I guess. When I was employed by the probation service, poetry was a kind of alternative life. It wasn't an escape from reality – I don't think driving around Manchester looking at babies with cigarette burns on their arms is any more or less real than writing at a desk – but it allowed a part of myself to exist that the Home Office didn't really recognise. Sometimes events at work became incidents within poems, and the language of convicts, solicitors and medics did find its way into the writing. In that sense, work was fuel to the poetry, although I'm convinced that if I'd been spending my days in another atmosphere or environment I would still have been writing at the same pace, even on the same themes, though of course the explicit subject matter and the vocabulary and the personnel of the poems would have been different.

But I also remember days when my brain was just too full to think about poetry, particularly days when I'd been working with words – writing court reports or case notes. Because of that, I tend to think that a job like school-teaching or proof-reading would really strangle my poetry. Having to be locked onto letters all day would take all the pleasure out of it and wouldn't give me the space to let my mind wander. When I talk about writing, I'm really talking about thinking, not putting pen to paper. A job that's stimulating but doesn't bag all your thinking time could be useful in the long run.

5. *Do you think the State or any other institution should do more for writers?*

I don't think that writers are owed a living by the State. It's difficult to argue the case without sounding reactionary, but I think writers have to strike a relationship with society on lots of levels, and one of those levels is financial. Even the shaman has to cure a patient every once in a while, and if a person has the neck to call him or herself a writer, let alone a poet, then they must seek to strike a bargain with the world and the people they hope to write for. Poetry is connected with the root conditions of being alive, and one aspect of that is survival. There are, of course, examples of good and even great writers who have lived and died in poverty, but there are more examples of writers who have remained poor because of the quality of their work and who haven't taken the hint. As for all the great poems that failed to be written because of hardship – well, it's difficult to argue on behalf of the non-existent. Good writing will find a means – I really believe that.

That isn't to say that the State shouldn't help out. Writing isn't a charity case, but it is special in that language lies at the root of all art, especially in modern times when a work of art is merited mainly by the dialogue and discussion that comes with it, especially in its written-down form (i.e. description and criticism). There is a level of funding and support which will always be inadequate in the sense that there is an apparently limitless number of people who fancy themselves as writers, even if they haven't been made aware of it yet.

6. *Are you satisfied with your own solution of the problem and have you any specific advice to give to young people who wish to earn their living by writing?*

It tends to be a day-to-day thing. This morning I might be happy because I'm doing what I most enjoy, tomorrow I might be pissed off because I'm having to do something silly or uncomfortable or unnatural or unconnected to earn a few pounds. It would be wrong of me to complain, given that I have managed to make a go of it and that I owe money to nobody. But I'm still baffled by the number of people who expect writers to do something for nothing. I don't know if it was intended as an irony, but payment for this very article is £200 of Waterstone's book tokens, and most writers I know need another two-hundred quids-worth of books in the house like they need another hole in their arse.

My advice to the young and innocent is to write the work, then see what comes. But don't bank on it. I'd say if it's money you're interested in, there are millions of easier ways to fame and fortune, and most of them wide open to the ignorant and untalented.

SIMON ARMITAGE *is the author of five collections of poetry, including* Kid, Book of Matches *and* The Dead Sea Poems. *The* Sunday Times *'Young Writer of the Year' in 1993, he has been shortlisted for the Whitbread Poetry Award three times and was voted 'Most Promising New Poet' for the Forward Poetry Prize in 1992. His most recent collection of poems,* CloudCuckooLand, *was published in September 1997.*

Beryl Bainbridge

1. *How much do you think a writer needs to live on?*

I had my first book published in 1967 by the 'New Authors' Hutchinson imprint. I received £25. For the next ten years, eight books on, my income was as follows – £7. 10 shillings alimony for self and two children, plus, lest you're weeping, a three-storied house in Camden Town, mortgage paid for six years, no advances and income of £3,600 a year. This sum increased in 1975 to £72 a week, plus family allowance for three children. From 1982 onwards I became rich, earning from journalism etc. over £9,000 a year. The last decade has seen a meteoric rise in my finances – culminating on average in excess of £35,000 a year. I can't say we did without in the lean years. More money just makes you think you need more. If I hadn't earned more I dare say I wouldn't have noticed being hard up.

2. *Do you think a serious writer can earn this sum by his writing, and if so, how?*

I don't quite understand what is meant by the word serious.

Anyone who writes takes his so-called 'work' seriously – but no, serious books don't sell well.

3. *If not, what do you think is the most serious occupation for him?*

In the old days – Jane Austen, the Brontë sisters – women got on with the dusting. The chaps either drank themselves to death, or relied on their wives, which seems reasonable. As for now, the men should go into gardening or poetry circles, and the ladies into presenting chat shows or cookery programmes. Either that or both should apply for employment at Marks and Sparks and scribble away in the evenings.

4. *Do you think literature suffers from the diversion of a writer's energy into other employment or is enriched by it?*

First, I think there should have been a comma after employment. Second, or perhaps secondly, I think writers are definitely impoverished by remaining incarcerated in their word-processor garrets. After a time, one stops meeting or knowing normal people.

5. *Do you think the State or any other institution should do more for writers?*

Absolutely not. Who needs writers?

6. *Are you satisfied with your own solution of the problem and have you any specific advice to give to young people who wish to earn their living by writing?*

I'm satisfied, but have no advice. I never expected to earn a living from writing and can't understand the source of the expectation. You either want to write or you don't. On second thoughts, the young scribbler should read and copy those he admires. Students used to do this in art schools – a process now abandoned, with lamentable results.

BERYL BAINBRIDGE *is the author of fifteen novels, as well as two travel books and five plays for stage and television. She has been shortlisted for the Booker Prize four times – for* The Dressmaker *(1973),* The Bottle Factory Outing *(1974),* An Awfully Big Adventure *(1989) and* Every Man for Himself *(1996) – and won the Whitbread Novel Award in 1977 with* Injury Time.

Julian Barnes

1. *How much do you think a writer needs to live on?*

The same as everyone else; that's to say, anything from a monkish £5,000 p.a. to a well-heeled professional's £100,000. It depends on temperament, social expectation, drug use, number of children, and so on. Does having too little money harm a writer? Yes, just as it harms non-writers. So does having too much; but that's less often a problem.

2. *Do you think a serious writer can earn this sum by his writing, and if so, how?*

For a while, with talent and luck. But you would have to be exceedingly vain or exceedingly foolish to set up as a writer and think that your art will sustain you until death. When I started reading seriously, Angus Wilson was one of our most acclaimed literary novelists. By the time I became a writer myself he was a knight. Not long afterwards, I remember being asked to contribute to an emergency fund to help sustain him. All surveys show that most writers earn far less than enough to live on.

3. *If not, what do you think is the most suitable second occupation for him?*

An over-paid, under-stretching job which leaves you free at the times when your brain is at its most creative. In the eighteenth century aristocrats supposedly advertised for hermits. Not anymore. Ideally, you need a job which takes you far away from the study. But being a brickie would consume too much energy; being a surgeon too much time.

4. *Do you think literature suffers from the diversion of a writer's energy into other employments or is enriched by it?*

It depends what sort of writer you are and how much energy you have.

5. *Do you think the State or any other institution should do more for writers?*

I'd put the emphasis the other way round. Writers should keep their distance from the state. They should be wary of hand-outs when they are young and honours when they are old. Even the most benign state is fundamentally coercive. If a writer were paid a salary by a transnational, readers would correctly view him or her with suspicion. What's the quid pro quo, they would ask. The State properly pays Public Lending Right, which is merely recompense for money semi-stolen; and the State should offer pensions to elderly writers who have fallen on hard times and aren't able to produce any more; then there is no question of a quo for the quid. Of course, writers might still think of refusing such charity, if only to maintain the principle that Art is greater than the State.

6. *Are you satisfied with your own solution of the problem and have you any specific advice to give to young people who wish to earn their living by writing?*

I don't think about a 'solution' to a 'problem' except on a day-to-day, book-by-book basis. A writer's life is fundamentally different from that of a salary-slave. You pay for the greater liberty with greater anxiety. Every day of your life you are freelance; you can't coast; you can't predict the depth or longevity of your talent; and given your improved personal longevity, you must expect still to be

alive when your talent has run out. The case of V. S. Pritchett, whose
first reading agreement with *The New Yorker* was still being annually
renewed when he was in his early nineties, is egregious. You are
more likely to end up (as one well-known 1960s novelist did)
receiving your last Christmas dinner from the Sally Army. But then
the career of a writer like Pritchett is almost unimaginable
nowadays. Publishers are much less willing to help build a writer
over decades – three strikes and you're out seems to be the rule.

So my advice to young writers would be: don't do it unless you
really want to; don't do it expecting that it will support you; don't do
it expecting that anyone will particularly like what you do; don't do
it imagining that once your talent has been revealed, the world will
conclude that it owes you a living; don't do it to mend some hole in
your life or purge yourself of some pain; don't do it unless you
believe, utterly, that making art is the most important thing there is;
don't do it assuming that the result will ever satisfy you. And finally:
don't take advice from older writers – they're only talking to
themselves. It's different for you. You're starting afresh. The world
awaits. Go for it.

JULIAN BARNES *is the author of eight works of fiction, including*
Metroland, A History of the World in 10 $\frac{1}{2}$ Chapters, Talking it
Over *and* Flaubert's Parrot, *for which he was awarded the* Prix Medicis.
Letters from London, *a collection of his articles on British culture and
politics written for* The New Yorker, *was published in 1995. His new book,*
England, England, *will be published in September 1998.*

Melvyn Bragg

1. *How much do you think a writer needs to live on?*

A writer needs as much as makes it possible to do the writing. The sum of money involved will differ widely. But a rough guide would be that it approximate to that of the writer's friends. When I started on my first (unpublished) novel in 1961–2, I was earning £625 a year. That was the going income of those I knew both in London and Cumberland. I earned nothing from my writing. By 1965, when I published my first novel, I was up to £1,050, married with a child. £150 advance was very welcome but it was not a livelihood. Being desperate for money is no use to anyone except, possibly and rarely, a writer who might just turn that desperation into words which would not otherwise have been produced. Twenty years on I began to earn, from writing, approximately what my friends earned from 'working'.

2. *Do you think a serious writer can earn this sum by his writing, and if so, how?*

Some 'serious writers' by Connolly's definition can and do make a living from their writing. Not many, and those few are a very small percentage of those who write professionally. But there are enough of them to show that it can be done. The answer to the question – how do they do it? – has to be simple: the public wants to buy their books in sufficient quantities. It is of course also true that many more 'serious writers' do not earn anything like a decent living from the writing they do.

3. *If not, what do you think is the most suitable second occupation for him?*

There is no 'suitable' occupation for a writer. Some work in banks, some work on boats, some roam the world, some stick at universities, some graze in the media, some live off others, some cadge, some inherit, some are held up by invisible wires. Anything that brings in what used to be called 'the necessary' and leaves time for the writing would be a suitable occupation.

4. *Do you think literature suffers from the diversion of a writer's energy into other employments or is enriched by it?*

This depends on the writer. You can construct any case you want by taking models from the past. Great writers have been heavily involved in other employment and one can only conclude, because of the quality of their work, that they have been enriched by it. Others have lashed themselves to the mast and equally have been enriched by that solitary obsession. Many have begun by being employed and writing and sometimes ended up solely writing – not always with the happiest results.

From my own experience, I think that if you are lucky enough to light on work you enjoy with people you like then that can be both energising and enriching. Just as work you hate can drain energy, so work you love can increase it. I do not think that the benefit of employment is necessarily direct – you do not automatically put the material of your work into your books. But, for a novelist especially, I think, to be part of a working society can be an education as well as a living.

5. *Do you think the State or any other institution should do more for writers?*

The State supports so many deserving and undeserving people that I do not see why writers should be left out. The problem is to prove that a writer is a writer by State rules. The Arts Council grapples with that, loses a few, wins a few. Money can disappear into the old pals' pockets and it can miss out a crying need. Performance is easier to justify, and playwrights – as part of that – are easier to subsidise. How and why to get help to the beginner, the poet or the novelist, has exercised many wise heads and we are no nearer a definition or a solution. I worked on the Arts Council to make sure that writers received grants and bursaries, but never applied for one myself. I just thought I had to get on with it. That, though, is a personal and limited testimony. The State always could do more – but how and how much will remain debatable.

6. *Are you satisfied with your own solution of the problem and have you any specific advice to give to young people who wish to earn their living by writing?*

No, I don't suppose anyone is. The only advice I could possibly give to young people is to keep going. If you do, then you may sooner or later get what you inevitably need – a break. And finally, nobody else forces you to do it.

MELVYN BRAGG *is a prolific author and a mainstay of British television and radio. He became Controller of Arts at London Weekend Television in 1990 and Director of LWT Productions in 1992. Editor and Presenter of the* South Bank Show *since 1978, he is the presenter of Radio 4's* Start the Week, *is the author of fifteen novels and has also written non-fiction, screenplays, films and musicals. On* Giants' Shoulders, *the book of his recent Radio 4 series, was published in March 1998.*

A. S. Byatt

1. *How much do you think a writer needs to live on?*

The answer to this question depends entirely on whether the writer in question has dependents – children, partner, or elderly relatives. And on whether he or she can get research grants, needs libraries etc. A young, solitary writer can make do on very little, but some changes of place and experience are necessary. I remember panicking in 1984 when I gave up university teaching and telling Iris Murdoch I should never get back to earning the £13,000 a year I got from that. (I was worried about the pension, too). She assured me that after a year or two, I should. I did. £20,000 a year would be more comfortable, I think.

2. *Do you think a serious writer can earn this sum by his writing, and if so, how?*

I fear most writers do not find it easy to make as much as that. There seems to be an increasing gap between those serious writers who have a steady readership and sales, and those who are still searching for these things. Individual writers are not helped by the great number of books published and the increasingly short shelf-life of new ones in bookshops. It helps to develop skills as a journalist, and as a radio and TV performer, though radio and television pay so little that they will not make a vast difference. I think really serious writers know what they want to say, and how to say it, but it also helps to be a serious reader, to keep an eye on what readers are interested in, to talk in bookshops to readers, if given the chance. Skills as a performing artist, almost unknown when I set out, at least among novelists, do now bring in small pockets of fees and increase sales, and have become required of established writers. In the end, the performing interferes with, and inhibits the writing, thus reducing the income again.

3. *If not, what do you think is the most suitable second occupation for him?*

In my early years as a writer, I found that teaching literature – to art students, in adult classes, at universities – was enormously enriching. This was largely because of the literature itself – the fierce thinking, the multifarious rhythms of the language, the sense that literature was real, and mattered. Recent critical movements have made that option less attractive – less and less time is spent on literature and more and more on theories of literature, which is exciting, but not nearly so good for one's work as a writer. There is the further problem that good teaching is very draining and exhausting. And the further problem that the great writers of the past, and even more, those of the present, can be daunting and depressing, rather than challenging, depending on one's mood and the state of one's inventiveness and confidence.

I would now incline to gardening. I know an artist who gains a great deal in his work from earning a living as a gardener and garden designer. It is quiet, physical, thoughtful and interesting.

Publishing, jobs on newspapers, the BBC etc. I suspect are not the best work. One will end up inhibited and writing narcissistic media narratives.

4. *Do you think literature suffers from the diversion of a writer's energy into other employments or is enriched by it?*

I think literature is on the whole enriched by writers doing other things than writing. There are too many books and too many writers and too much repetition. In the nineteenth century writers knew the whole of the world they wrote about – doctors, lawyers and bankers were easily recognisable and science, philosophy, politics and art were all discussed in the same reviews. Now most writers do not know what most people are doing and thinking about. A man at the ICA once challenged David Lodge and myself with the observation that when he was young he was interested in the media, academe and the kitchen, but now he was not. Novelists, he said, were on the whole restricted to these settings. He was interested in multi-national companies and science: novelists were not. His comments aroused some indignation in the audience, but I agreed with him. It is odd that thriller writers do get to know the worlds of other people's work and preoccupations whilst 'serious' writers (novelists) on the whole, do not.

5. *Do you think the State or any other institution should do more for writers?*

After much reflection, I incline to the unfashionable view that subsidising writers directly is not very helpful. Most writers, in practice, cannot afford to give up their secondary incomes to live briefly on grants designed to buy writing time. They dare not risk losing them permanently. I think things like the Royal Literary Fund are very important, since most writers cannot afford to take care of pensions or medical contingencies. I also think that the subsidy of journals, anthologies etc., which publish what writers write and *pay them for what they have written* is very important. Marvellous short stories are being written in this country and there is almost nowhere to read them – the annual *New Writing*, which is subsidised by the British Council, fulfils a real need. I think the Public Lending Right gives both financial and moral encouragement, and a sense of justice, to writers, and I think subsidy spent on our once wonderful, now struggling public library service – subsidy specifically for books, not for music – would make an enormous difference. Such subsidy would encourage both writers and readers, and sustain the literature, which is the art in which we excel.

6. *Are you satisfied with your own solution of the problem and have you any specific advice to give to young people who wish to earn their living by writing?*

My own solution to the problem has been paradoxical. I spent many years exhausting myself teaching at university in order to pay for child-care etc. and now suspect that if I had had the courage of my convictions I should have been much richer, much earlier, by writing more concentratedly. On the other hand, I think the teaching, and the reading, enriched my work as a writer. It would all be all right if one had two life-times. You learn how to do it, and it's almost over.

Advice to the young:

Read. Read everything you can, literature, science, popular nonsense, politics. Keeping your soul pure and uncontaminated by other people's thoughts and art makes you boring and paradoxically just like everyone else.

When you are young, take on everything that's offered. Apply your intelligence to techniques; learn quickly *how much thought and style* you can get into 200, or 600, or 1000 words and do not write essays and painfully reduce them. Learn to avoid writing blocks by making skeletons. Subsidiary writings should be done fast or they'll eat your life. Never write anything you are ashamed of. It haunts you.

When you are old, and it's working, learn the opposite lesson. Learn to say no. You get into the habit of thinking no one will ever ask you again, and after a time that's not true. After a certain age, it's all a battle with the end. And you need to have written what you could and should have written when it comes.

A. S. BYATT *is the author of thirteen works of fiction and non-fiction. Amongst her fiction titles are the novels* The Virgin in the Garden, Babel Tower *and* Possession, *winner of the 1990 Booker Prize, and the short story collections* The Matisse Stories *and* The Djinn and the Nightingale's Eye. *Non-fiction works include* Wordsworth and Coleridge in their Time *and* Passions of the Mind. *A former Chairman of the Society of Authors and a Fellow of the Royal Society of Literature, A. S. Byatt was appointed a C.B.E. in 1990 for her work as a writer.*

Jonathan Coe

1. *How much do you think a writer needs to live on?*

At the time of writing, the average yearly income for full-time employment in Great Britain is £19,115. I don't see why writers should expect any less than that. Most of them deserve a good deal more.

2. *Do you think a serious writer can earn this sum by his writing, and if so, how?*

Publishing is market-driven, and the market makes bizarre, random and unjust choices. I know serious writers who make a good living from their writing, mediocre writers who make a small fortune from it, talented writers who are struggling to survive and bad writers living in penury. There is no rhyme or reason to the present system. If you're lucky enough to hitch a ride on the latest fashionable bandwagon and happen to catch the attention of an editor with money to spend, you can make a few hundred thousand from one book. On the other hand, you might write a masterpiece which looks so unmarketable that it scares publishers off and either gets poorly published or not published at all. There's no correlation betwen literary merit and financial reward, so all you can do for the sake of your own sanity is to write the books you want to write, and hope that one day *somebody* with spending power will finally take a fancy to what you do: preferably the reading public – in which case, your well-being is temporarily secured – but failing that, a powerful editor or a film producer. It also helps if you're widely published overseas. Your income will double if you're published in America, and increase threefold if you're widely translated throughout Europe.

3. *If not, what do you think is the most suitable second occupation for him?*

Most fiction writers supplement their income with literary journalism. This is not good for the soul, although it has its financial attractions. Reviewers for Associated Newspapers (the *Evening Standard, Mail on Sunday,* etc.) can expect to be paid at least £1 a word for dishing out undemanding copy to middlebrow readers. One such review a week might therefore bring in £30,000 a year. Rupert Murdoch's News International papers pay slightly less than this, while the *Guardian* and *Observer* – where serious writers might expect to feel more comfortable – a little less still. I did review for the best part of a decade, full of youthful enthusiasm at first, then increasingly troubled by the thought of making snap (and sometimes hostile) judgments on books which had taken people years to write, until financial circumstances allowed me to give it up. I dare say I would go back to it if times got hard, and if anyone would have me.

4. *Do you think literature suffers from the diversion of a writer's energy into other employments or is enriched by it?*

It's true that insight into the ordinary working lives of most people is not among the greatest strengths of the contemporary British writer. One solution would be for us all to take proper jobs for five years and discover a little more about what's really going on out there, so that we might get a few more novels with, say, the stinging authenticity of Jeff Torrington's *Swing Hammer Swing*. Of course, this won't happen: but it helps, at least, to have a circle of family and friends who keep you grounded, and remind you that outside the circuit of academia, bookchat and reading tours, there is a life going on which demands to be attended to and written about. There can be some benefit in taking on other work during those fallow periods when ideas are lying dormant or slowly germinating, but any kind of distraction – reviewing, teaching, scriptwriting, whatever – is a disaster when you're deep into the most intense phase of writing a novel.

5. *Do you think the State or any other institution should do more for writers?*

I've invariably been turned down for any state grants that I've applied for, so naturally I have a rather jaundiced view. But I know very well that committees can be whimsical things, so it's no surprise that the few meagre Arts Council grants are often handed out to writers who never go on to fulfil whatever promise was recognised. Occasionally, though, one or two genuinely gifted and struggling writers come through the system almost by accident, and I suppose that makes the whole process worthwhile.

It seems positively eccentric to talk about 'the State' at all in these post-welfare, Blairite days, but I do believe that there should be one state-owned publishing house. It should be non-profit-making, and run by a single enlightened editor (supported by an army of well-paid readers, to wade through the floodtides of manuscripts it would attract). Its remit would be to publish books of high quality – not just fiction – which were considered unviable by the commercial houses, and for which it would pay reasonable but not outrageous advances. That way, a home might be found for the more difficult, experimental or arcane novels, poems and essays which at the moment don't have a hope in hell of getting properly published. The sort of thing that Harvill or Marion Boyars are trying to do, only on an absolutely solid financial footing. This would be a far more useful state intervention, in my view, than the allocation of Arts Council grants to individual writers.

6. *Are you satisfied with your own solution of the problem and have you any specific advice to give to young people who wish to earn their living by writing?*

'Satisfied' is not the right word. I consider myself, at the moment, to be very lucky. The Gods of the literary marketplace are smiling on me, I get good advances, I've found a reasonable-sized public, and I can choose exactly what sort of work I want to do. It's taken me about ten years to get to this point and, if luck persists, might take a few more years to topple of it. This puts me in a tiny and privileged minority. I could name a dozen supremely talented novelists for whom financial insecurity is a daily fact of life. No cause for satisfaction there.

Young writers should go into the business with realistic expectations. The literary world is driven by market forces and fashion, and if your work doesn't happen to be in harmony with these factors, you will have a hard time. And yet to write anything other than what you want or need to write is pointless, boring and soul-destroying. Pay no attention to fairytales about new authors' multi-million pound windfalls: it happens occasionally, and for some reason is the only kind of literary story the newspapers are interested in reporting, but it won't happen to you. (I was paid a few hundred pounds for my first novel.) Make it your target to be earning a modest living after a few years and for the rest, let the work itself be its own reward.

JONATHAN COE *is the author of five novels, including* What a Carve Up! *which won the 1995 John Llewellyn Rhys Prize and, in France the 1996* Prix du Meilleur Livre Etranger. House of Sleep, *his most recent novel, was published in 1997.*

Fred D'Aguiar

1. *How much do you think a writer needs to live on?*

Writers are said to be notoriously greedy when it comes to money. Apparently, they talk about nothing else except the size of their contracts. Greediness apart, a writer's needs are as crucial as the next person's. Whatever the average wage is for a top-notch civil servant to function adequately, that amount should be paid to the writer in order to free up his time and energy. Because a writer never stops writing, awake or asleep, half-starved or obese, he is easily ignored. But a society does so at its peril, its cultural life may atrophy in exact correlation with the misfortune or otherwise of its writers (and other artists).

2. *Do you think a serious writer can earn this sum by his writing, and if so, how?*

Too few serious writers generate enough cash from the sweat of their brow. A handful of writers command bumper advances and fat royalty cheques. For the rest of us the covenant with the muse is a less rewarding one. Writers require a long-term investment in them on several fronts before their work bears fruit. Even so, there's no guarantee that the fruit will be edible. Pedestrian scripts may still be the result of State sponsorship. But the community of writers is a happier one when the State pays attention to their plight. With State involvement the idea of writers as a valued wing of the country's cultural life is writ large. In the absence of creative State interference writers feel at the mercy of the market. A little notoriety on the part of the writer helps; some aspect of the writer's public personality that can cross-over into the awful, draconian world of print and broadcast culture. But this is too rare to promote as viable.

3. *If not, what do you think is the most suitable second occupation for him?*

Any job that pays well should suffice. Most writers do something other than write in order to survive. Part-time work of some kind but with a full-time salary (a job whose pay is topped up by an Arts Council subsidy for as long as the writer shows up for work!) sounds ideal. More writers should work for the Arts Council. There should be a Minister for each segment of the various art forms supported by boards made up of the relevant practitioners.

4. *Do you think literature suffers from the diversion of a writer's energy into other employments or is enriched by it?*

I've heard the argument that poets are born not made and therefore the flow of poems cannot be stopped by placing that divinely inspired creature in something so trifling as poverty. Then I try to imagine Yeats' *Collected Poems* without Lady Gregory's patronage and I see that a large number of the poems might be absent from it. In other words, nature, for all its munificence, still can be trumped by an adverse nurture. Most work for money is drudgery, something of a ball-breaker, hateful and brain-numbing. It does seem to subtract from writing. Of course, a writer who wants to say something urgently will find a way to get his message out even if he were incarcerated on Devil's Island. But why should he be punished for choosing a vocation no one in a position to help cares about?

5. *Do you think the State or any other institution should do more for writers?*

Much, much more. Once the writer declares his serious intent in a few published short stories or poems or, if lucky, a novel or a produced play, then the State should shower him with material comforts to facilitate more art; travel grants, awards, that sort of thing. I see the State and Arts Council as facilitators: they cannot make writers write more or better but they can go some way towards ameliorating the conditions under which writers function.

6. *Are you satisfied with your own solution of the problem and have you any specific advice to give to young people who wish to earn their living by writing?*

My solution is something of an accident: a series of time-consuming hits and misses during the 1980s – readings where the fee sometimes depended on the number of people who turned up or travel to and from gigs that ate up a good part of two days, and an extra day to recover, for £75 (I managed a lot of my reading and writing on trains) – before finding something satisfactory now as a teacher of writing at a university. I consider a lot of what I do for bread hugely diversionary. What a shame! How many poems, stories am I losing along the way?! My advice to the young is that they should read everything and write every day, but also procure a parallel skill, art or craft aimed specifically at paying the bills (the less taxing the better); and since the young are energetic, they should lobby the Arts Council to set up an extensive programme of writers' bursaries, travel grants, awards, pensions and any other manner of manna.

Born in London in 1960, FRED D'AGUIAR *is a poet, novelist and playwright. His three collections of poetry –* Mama Dot, Airy Hall *and* British Subjects *– have brought him many prizes, including the T. S. Eliot Prize for poetry, and his first novel,* The Longest Memory, *won the Whitbread First Novel Award. His latest book, the long poem* Bill of Rights, *was published in March 1998.*

William Dalrymple

1. *How much do you think a writer needs to live on?*

How long is a piece of string?

2. *Do you think a serious writer can earn this sum by his writing, and if so, how?*

If the myth of the writer in the garret was ever true, it is certainly misleading today. Writers love to whinge as much as anyone else, but since the quantum leap in publishers advances during the 1980s, it has certainly been possible to make a reasonable living as a writer – as long as what you are writing sells reasonably well, and as long as you work hard enough to produce a major book every two or three years. None of the professional writers I know live in poverty. There are certainly exceptions, but most of us seem to get by fine with incomes comparable to – say – averagely-successful journalists, i.e. around £20–40,000 a year, of which at least a quarter comes from journalism and reviewing.

Admittedly this is partly through a process of shake-down: those writers I know who didn't make it by the age of 35 or so have tended to give up and become chartered accountants or whatever.

3. *If not, what do you think is the most suitable second occupation for him?*

Usually the question doesn't arise: most real writers – and certainly those who are any good – are by definition unemployable. Writing is a school for selfishness and self-obsession. Once you've been used to being your own boss, getting out of bed when you want, writing about what interests you, in your own home, while listening to your own music, the idea of working for anyone else becomes inconceivable. Speaking for myself, I've never held down a job for longer than six months. The longer you've been a writer, the more unemployable you become.

4. *Do you think literature suffers from the diversion of a writer's energy into other employments or is enriched by it?*

That said, the worst thing that can happen to a writer is to be cut off from his inspiration and from real life. It is much more dangerous to be cloistered for ever in your study than to be made to leave it occasionally. To be forced to get out of the house and go off and – say – write a magazine article keeps the juices flowing. If Chaucer and Burns hadn't been customs men, if Trollope hadn't worked in his post office, would their work have been so full of so many extraordinary characters? But extra-curricular activities should be strictly kept in check; more than anything else a writer needs time.

5. *Do you think the State or any other institution should do more for writers?*

The state should never become a writer's paymaster, though it is always nice to be boosted now and again with an Arts Council prize or travel grant. And while it would be nice to be exempt of tax like our colleagues in Ireland, I can't really think of any good reason why we should be if factory workers and school teachers are not. One thing that does always irritate me, however, is the attitude of the state to giving honours to writers. What does it say about a country that it showers knighthoods on dull-as-ditch Tory back-benchers, Foreign Office bores and brain-dead luvvies, but ignores its writers and artists – except, so it seems, for the odd science fiction scribbler or one semi-literate, notoriously mendacious and politically-ambitious 'writer' of blockbusters? The only serious writers I can think of who have received any state recognition recently are V. S. Naipaul and Tom Stoppard. This is one clear field where the state could show that it values the work that writers are doing.

6. *Are you satisfied with your own solution of the problem and have you any specific advice to give to young people who wish to earn their living by writing?*

I can think of no more wonderful life than that of the author. Every morning as I sit down at my desk I can't quite believe how lucky I am not to have to go to an office and be told to do something dull by a man in a suit. If authors are not as well paid as lawyers and bankers, so be it. Writers these days have no reason to complain and an awful lot to be grateful for. As for advice, I would simply urge anyone who wants to be a writer to be brave, take the leap of faith and work hard to make it happen. If you can find a way of making a living as a writer you are lucky beyond all riches.

WILLIAM DALRYMPLE'*s first travel book,* In Xanadu, *was published in 1990 and was followed by* City of Djinns, *which won the 1994 Thomas Cook Travel Book Award and the* Sunday Times *Young British Writer of the Year Award. His third book,* From the Holy Mountain, *was published in April 1998. He is currently writing a six-part television series on the buildings of the Raj for Channel 4.*

Jenny Diski

1. *How much do you think a writer needs to live on?*

However much it takes to allow the writer to lie awake in the early hours worrying about the writing rather than the gas bill. This is about the same, with allowances for circumstances – children, ageing parents and so forth – as should be available as a minimum for anyone to live on. Things don't look hopeful in either case.

2. *Do you think a serious writer can earn this sum by his writing, and if so, how?*

If a serious writer is one who is serious about writing, she will write even if she can't earn her living by it. If she also writes serious things, her chances of making a living at it are small and depend a great deal on luck, fashion and contacts and productivity.

3. *If not, what do you think is the most suitable second occupation for him?*

Personally, I would be delighted to be offered a job as a lighthouse keeper. Other suitable occupations include monk/nun, gate keeper, game keeper, poacher, kept woman/man, lollipop person. Otherwise, it looks as if comedian, movie star and supermodel are the best career bets at present. Standard jobs in business, say publishing, used to look like secure bases from which to finance the iffy prospects of writing. These days, I note with a small degree of amused satisfaction, such professions are no more reliable than freelancing.

4. Do you think literature suffers from the diversion of a writer's energy into other employments or is enriched by it?

It's very hard to write a book if you are distracted by having to earn a living. Still, a certain tension may be useful to writers. Journalism is difficult. The required tone is so slick that real writing may die of asphyxia. It would be best, though extremely difficult right now, to avoid writing a column about your life, even or especially if it is fictional; and be very cautious about reviewing other people's fiction.

5. Do you think the State or any other institution should do more for writers?

I've often wondered whether I wouldn't have been much relieved and not greatly damaged to have received an annual salary from a publisher during the early stages. A decent sum of money (see 1.), coming in regularly, say for a period of five years, in return for the rights to any books written. Authors demand advances they can't earn back when they sense that there is no long-term commitment to them as writers, only a calculated guess at profit margins from book to book. I recall being told by a highly paid editor who was buying the paperback rights of my second novel for not much money that it was important for a writer 'to grow slowly'. At the time I had a pile of household bills that had no interest at all in my literary growth rate. I dislike the use of prizes for money, which turn writers into racehorses and demand they be in public competition with each other. Private competition is bad enough. They are a cheap and cheerful way for publishers to get publicity without having to lay out any money on advertising. A grant system based on need seems like a better idea. Established writers can get a medal if they must, but not £20,000 they don't remotely need.

6. *Are you satisfied with your own solution of the problem and have you any specific advice to give to young people who wish to earn their living by writing?*

I am currently deliriously happy with my situation, which is that I can live by writing. My delirium is slightly curtailed by the knowledge that the present state of affairs is unlikely to last, and I nonetheless scour the small ads for lighthouse-keeping opportunities. Young writers would be well advised to marry wisely if not well, or find a lighthouse.

JENNY DISKI *is the author of seven novels* – Nothing Natural, Rainforest, Like Mother, Then Again, Happily Ever After, Monkey's Uncle *and* The Dream Mistress – *as well as a collection of short stories,* The Vanishing Princess. *Her first work of non-fiction,* Skating to Antarctica, *was published in* 1997.

Helen Dunmore

1. *How much do you think a writer needs to live on?*

A writer should take great care never to be old, ill, pregnant or depended upon, or she will find that she needs just as much money as anybody else.

2. *Do you think a serious writer can earn this sum by his writing, and if so, how?*

A novelist can live by writing, but very few poets will be able to do so, no matter how good they are or how well-regarded their work may be. A poet may be very much in demand to give workshops or readings, but receive relatively little from royalties. The bizarre situation then arises when a professional writer may spend years encouraging others to write, but is unable to buy enough writing time for himself or herself.

Most writers have odd earning patterns, compared to people in other professions. The writer might begin with ten years or so of learning to write, and an early publication or two. These are unlikely to make much money. At this point the writing is subsidised by another job, or another person. If the writer is fortunate, and his or her reputation takes off, there may be some years of good earnings – possibly even high earnings. Then tastes may change. The money slows, or even stops. There's no pension or sick pay, or holiday pay, of course. It's quite an interesting exercise to average out the income of writers *from writing* over their lifetimes, and it puts breathless newspaper stories about high advances into perspective.

3. *If not, what do you think is the most suitable second occupation for him?*

Any occupation which earns money and doesn't completely swallow up the imagination, or physically exhaust the writer. But often it's necessary to take jobs which do one or both of these. There's a lot of compromise involved. I've sometimes thought that to be a doctor is a good occupation for a poet (I'm thinking of Dannie Abse, for example). But it takes a rare individual to manage two professions.

Young women writers often end up with one unpaid occupation (child-rearing), one which isn't making much money yet (writing), and a day-job to earn money. It's not impossible, but it's wearing. It makes me want to question Cyril Connolly upon his remark that the pram in the hall is the 'enemy of promise'. Enemy of whose promise?

4. *Do you think literature suffers from the diversion of a writer's energy into other employments or is enriched by it?*

This is a difficult one, and I think I can only answer it personally. I don't think energy is a given quantity which gets used up like a box of tea-bags. When writing is going well it creates its own momentum. As for diversions, sometimes they're frustrating and they destroy books, but not always. When I wrote my novel *A Spell of Winter* I was pregnant, and then looking after a new baby. I think these circumstances enriched the book rather than impoverished it. But on the other hand, by that time I was able to afford part-time help with the baby, and without it the book could not have been written. And I was only able to afford that help because I was already earning money from writing . . . so I haven't got any conclusions, except a feeling of profound gratitude that the whole thing didn't fall apart.

I find that reviewing works well alongside writing fiction. Teaching is more problematic, because it tends to use up the same kind of energy as writing.

5. *Do you think the State or any other institution should do more for writers?*

Relatively little State arts funding goes directly to writers, artists, musicians and dancers to enable them to buy time in order to do their work. A writer, dancer or musician usually lives on a fraction of the amount it takes to pay an employee of a Regional Arts Board, for example. Such an employee will expect a living wage, along with sick pay, pension, holiday pay etc. It is humiliating when writers have to jump through endless hoops for the smallest grant or financial award: I'm talking here about very detailed and demanding application forms, which ask for full disclosure of financial circumstances with no guarantee of privacy. Perhaps writers' organisations such as The Society of Authors or The Writers' Guild could be entrusted with more State arts funding, in order to make grants directly to writers.

Apart from State funding, there are organisations such as the Authors' Licensing and Collecting Society, which ensures that authors receive the money due to them from electronic rights, photocopying, European broadcasting etc. It would be good if more writers knew about such organisations, and belonged to them, because copyright is not something to be taken for granted. It's usually under attack in one way or another. Again, money from Public Lending Right is something we only receive because of a long, vigorous campaign by writers.

6. *Are you satisfied with your own solution of the problem and have you any specific advice to give to young people who wish to earn their living by writing?*

I am happy in my life as a writer. However, I can't congratulate myself on 'my solution', because the career of a writer is so uncertain, and so is the income. At the moment my books sell, and I am delighted by this and grateful for it, but it would be stupid to count on it for the future. Perhaps a trickle of PLR to buy thermal underwear in my eighties . . .

The great thing about writing is that you don't need much money to buy the materials – compared to a sculptor, say. And then the work can be reproduced an infinite number of times without any loss to the creator. It must hard for a painter to sell a painting and learn afterwards that it is sitting in a bank vault.

As for advising others, I don't think I would want to give general advice to younger writers. I'd rather look at a poem or short story, and talk about it with the writer. Or, on a more practical level, discuss which magazine might be good for a batch of poems, or which agent might be right for a particular first novel manuscript. When I started to publish, in my early twenties, I was very naive about how publishing worked, and about how to earn any sort of living from writing. I remember, for example, sending my only copy of a poem to Jon Silkin at *Stand*. When he discovered this on contacting me to discuss revisions, he pointed out quite gently that I 'must never do that again'.

I learned a lot about writing and money from other writers, but in a very informal way: through listening to despairing conversations in pubs about contracts, or through observing writers who saw no contradiction between their creativity and an efficient, sharp-witted management of their business affairs. It seems to me to be worth passing on whatever one can pass on without causing boredom or irritation. If advice is to be of any real use, it should be specific, and generous in its spirit.

HELEN DUNMORE *is a poet, novelist, short-story writer and children's novelist. Winner of the 1996 Orange Prize for fiction for her novel* A Spell of Winter, *she has also won many awards for her poetry. Her sixth and most recent collection,* Bestiary, *was shortlisted for the 1997 T. S. Eliot Prize for Poetry, and her fifth novel,* Your Blue-Eyed Boy, *will be published in May 1998.*

Paul Durcan

1. *How much do you think a writer needs to live on?*

A serious writer needs as much as any other serious artist. At the
moment, Antony Gormley is in the news on account of his Angel of
the North. Whatever Antony Gormley earns per annum would be
about right. A writer needs to have wings. Needs to be able to decide
in the morning to get out from under the low, grey cloud and fly to
Los Angeles to pray with an old friend and grab a cab to Malibu and
gaze at the Pacific.

   The notion that the writer should be a psychotic pauper in an
attic barking at the moon or a genius on heroin or drinking himself
to death in the corner bar is as ridiculous as it is nostalgic: a
nineteenth-century, bourgeois concept of how the artist should be
controlled and kept in check. In fact, the serious writer is also an
Angel of the North, forever spreading his or her Wings of Desire.
Writing is a vocation: a call to flying.

2. *Do you think a serious writer can earn this sum by his writing, and if
so, how?*

A serious poet has no chance of earning the necessary income. The
necessary angel – as Wallace Stevens may have said to Antony
Gormley's mother – requires the necessary wherewithal. The mother
of anxiety is poverty: and anxiety is the death of art. 'Poverty,' wrote
Patrick Kavanagh in *Self-Portrait*, 'has nothing to do with eating your
fill today: it is anxiety about what's going to happen next week.'

3. *If not, what do you think is the most suitable second occupation for him?*

As a writer, my chief preoccupation in life – apart from writing, and climbing mountains in search of beautiful women – is reading books. I see myself as first and last a reader who, in between my daily liturgy of book reading, attempts to write. Accordingly, the most suitable occupation for me would be conversing in public about the books I read, the paintings I see, the plays and films I attend. I have never been able to understand why newspaper editors, and television and radio producers, have not been beating my door down to pay me large sums of money for essays on my reading adventures, not to mention my sporting, my cinematic, my gallery, my theatre activities. The key word is 'essay'. Writing essays, or giving talks on literature and the other arts would be as congenial as it would be suitable: on the other hand, I regard writing blurbs, notices, advertisements, columns as wholly unsuitable, and as destructive as alcohol. The essay precludes bytes. The essay is all digression and parataxis. Inside every writer there is an A. J. P. Taylor aspiring to fly out of the window of your TV set and to instruct mankind. Oddly enough writers happen also to be storytellers.

4. *Do you think literature suffers from the diversion of a writer's energy into other employments or is enriched by it?*

Congenial employment enriches a writer's energy as well as his pocket. Unfortunately, all my employments have been uncongenial: stints as scullion, security guard, clerk, hack. Only my life as a Stellar Manipulator at the London Planetarium lived up to spiritual as well as financial expectations. Nor are an excess of public recitals to be recommended for either a writer's physical or financial well-being. The business of writers is writing.

5. *Do you think the State or any other institution should do more for writers?*

The State should always be doing more for writers. The State can never do enough: whether it is persecuting writers, as in Russia for the last two centuries; or in the Republic of Ireland, where the Arts Council provides writers, artists and composers with a basic, partial income.

6. *Are you satisfied with your own solution of the problem and have you any specific advice to give to young people who wish to earn their living by writing?*

After thirty-five years of hanging on by my fingertips in an effort to write poetry on a day-to-day basis, I consider myself steeped in luck to be still alive. I owe my life to certain women; to the Arts Council of the Republic of Ireland; to my readers; and to the hand of God. I do not believe in 'chance'. I believe in good politics; wise legislation; justice; love; and friendship.

When I behold a young person setting off down the mean streets of poetry, I feel at once thrilled and grief-stricken. I try to point them in the direction of Wallace Stevens. When all is said and done, I should like myself to be free of all stipends and bursaries and, instead, to be earning my own living as the weekly broadcaster of 'Letter From Art Street' or as Vice-President of Irish Life Insurance and to be dictating poems to my secretary. My dream – apart from winning the lottery – is to have a secretary. Meanwhile, to all would-be writers, I say: 'Consider Carver's Law of the Laundromat and decide: is this really the way you want to live?' (c.f. Raymond Carver, *Fires*, 1982.)

Writing poetry is my life but I would not recommend a poet's life to anyone. The price – as T. S. Eliot reflected – is too high. Or is it? That is the question.

Born in Dublin in 1944, PAUL DURCAN *is the author of fourteen collections of poetry, including* The Berlin Wall Café *(Poetry Book Society Choice, 1985),* O Westport in the Light of Asia Minor *and* Christmas Day. *In 1989 he received the Irish American Cultural Institute Poetry Award and in 1990 won the Whitbread Poetry Award with* Daddy, Daddy.

Alice Thomas Ellis

1. *How much do you think a writer needs to live on?*

About the same as anyone else. It all depends on the writer's
ambitions, appetites and responsibilities. A single person of modest
tastes and lifestyle could muddle by on £10,000, whereas a person
whose inclinations tend to the florid – theatre-going, foreign travel,
eating in restaurants, buying clothes from shops other than Oxfam
etc. – would need more in the region of £30,000, or limitless
amounts if he was extravagant or had a large family or families. Just
like everyone else. An impoverished writer might comfort himself
with the soothing reflection, given utterance by a thoughtful young
person, that there is a glamour attending the out-of-work artist
lacking in the life of the out-of-work plumber. The haunted-looking
creature in the bar who daily drags himself away from the
construction of his Novel (usually consisting of a synopsis and a
number of incoherent aperçus) can often persuade members of the
public to stand him a drink. Good-looking women can also benefit
in this way if their principles permit.

**2. *Do you think a serious writer can earn this sum by his writing, and if
so, how?***

I suppose by a 'serious writer' is meant a person who gets down to it
and does not mess about. A more appropriate word might be
'lucky'. I know too many talented and industrious writers who
cannot find a publisher to suggest that mere hard work is the route

to success. If you've done something frightful or are intimate with someone who's done something frightful, that seems to be a good start. Large sums are often paid to people in politics or sport who elect to turn their hand to literature. Journalism pays well if you can get a toehold in the richer papers or magazines and can afford to wait for the payment. If you can't, it doesn't. Fees vary enormously. Film and TV deals and foreign rights etc. (and the Public Lending Right) can add useful sums to the kitty of even the moderately successful writer. Luck again.

3. *If not, what do you think is the most suitable second occupation for him?*

How about politics or sport as a preparation? A number of excellent novelists have started off in advertising, a fine seedbed for fiction. Curiously enough, the best journalists seem to find it difficult to make the transition. Perhaps the most convenient occupation for the would-be writer (though not open to everyone) is that of housewife. It offers many opportunities to observe human nature closely and affords plenty of spare time when the children are asleep or have left home. I speak from experience. So don't all howl at once. I do not see how people who commute daily to work could do much else as well. A manual job would be preferable to a desk job, something that allows time for reflection and is not too taxing on the thought processes, which must be conserved for the epic. Women are better than men at doing a number of things at the same time, but there are limits. Men seem genuinely to need closed rooms and silence in order to write – unlike Jane Austen, for example.

4. *Do you think literature suffers from the diversion of a writer's energy into other employments or is enriched by it?*

On admittedly rather ageing evidence, the jobs of bar-tender, ordinary seaman (years before the mast), cattle-puncher, plongeur, grape-harvester etc. etc. seem to have been fruitful employment for writers in terms of experience, but things are rather different now. Travelling is good for writers of either sex but paid opportunities are fewer than they were. Obviously writers should have something to write about or they will be confined to the interior monologue, which can be tedious for the reader.

5. *Do you think the State or any other institution should do more for writers?*

I see no reason why the State, the taxpayer, should subsidise writers. (If there's any spare money around, nurses and teachers should get it.) The few writers I've known who have sulked at not getting special concessions and benefits have not been very good writers. One of them, a communist, wasn't even hard-up: he had an idea that there was something uniquely special about him and his chosen craft and he should be allowed particular status. He sought recognition rather than money, a sort of judicial approval rather than popular acclaim, although he'd have liked that too. A dangerous notion. Most institutions are either corrupt already, or open to corruption and given to nepotism. They might seek to use a writer for propaganda purposes or give preference to their chums. The writer should maintain independence. Publishers should, in their own eventual interests, be prepared to take risks and nurture new talent rather than give vast sums to established authors. They should sack the accountants and re-employ good editors.

On the other hand, large advances can be counterproductive. The stick is the best incentive. Humans, like donkeys once they've eaten the carrot, have a sense of false security and tend to lie down, while those with tender consciences worry about the responsibility of living up to expectations.

6. *Are you satisfied with your own solution of the problem and have you any specific advice to give to young people who wish to earn their living by writing?*

I can't complain. I suggest that young people who wish to earn a living by writing should be angry about something. Writing without an axe to grind is a boring business.

ALICE THOMAS ELLIS *is the author of twelve works of fiction, including* The 27th Kingdom *(which was shortlisted for the Booker Prize)*, Unexplained Laughter, The Inn at the Edge of the World *and* The Evening of Adam. *Her latest novel,* Fairy Tale, *was published in September 1997.*

Lucy Ellmann

1. *How much do you think a writer needs to live on?*

Writers need financial worries like they need soggy paper, inkless pens, uncomfortable desk-chairs and their own TV show. They need money troubles like they need toddlers round their feet, neighbours, incessant phone calls and CATS. They need them as much as they need a perpetual hankering for company, microwave popcorn or narcotics. They need them like they need an addiction to some time-consuming hobby like embroidery, muscle-building or computer-dating. They JUST DON'T NEED 'EM.

I suppose there's a remote chance that a prosperous writer might lose touch with the real world, start floating off, like someone in a Woody Allen musical, repeating old jokes and breaking into amateurish SONG without warning. Perhaps a writer can live too well to write well? What really happens to a writer given infinite access to SMOKED SALMON?

Actually, I think writers (like *everyone else*) need a minimum of £20,000 and a maximum of £50,000 a year. Anyone who earns more than that by writing should be physically restrained, big show-offs.

2. *Do you think a serious writer can earn this sum by his writing, and if so, how?*

Rarely. The serious writer is left to think seriously about putting his or her seriousness on hold whilst earning some serious money through journalism, teaching, waitressing or prostitution.

3. If not, what do you think is the most suitable second occupation for him?

Those mentioned above. Or inheritance. Dabbling with the stock market tends to become too engrossing (AND it's corrupt).

4. Do you think literature suffers from the diversion of a writer's energy into other employments or is enriched by it?

A novelist's time is best spent learning how to write novels. Or drinking martinis. One or the other. My fiction, as far as I can discern, in no way benefited from the despair and frustration that resulted from my many (occasionally lucrative) dealings with newspaper sub-editors. Journalism practically KILLED me (I was overjoyed to be fired).

5. Do you think the State or any other institution should do more for writers?

Of course. EVERYONE should do more for writers. They should be given discounts at bookshops, stationers, off-licences, restaurants, amusement arcades, swimming pools (for the inevitable back trouble) and chemists' shops (for the inevitable hypochondria).

I've never been given a fucking penny by the Arts Council and I'm *not happy about it.*

6. Are you satisfied with your own solution of the problem and have you any specific advice to give to young people who wish to earn their living by writing?

I had commissions for all three of my novels, though Penguin finally decided to call their last commission/advance an 'interest-free loan' and asked for it back! There is no publisher loyalty anymore. My current solution is to rely heavily on my charismatic agent, and my savings.

As for young writers, whenever possible I AVOID giving them advice. People never take my advice anyway.

LUCY ELLMANN *is the author of three novels, including* Sweet Desserts, *which won the Guardian Fiction Prize in 1988, and* Man or Mango, *which was published in March 1998. A regular reviewer for the* Guardian, Observer *and* Times Literary Supplement, *she has also been TV reviewer and a regular columnist for the* Independent on Sunday.

Sebastian Faulks

1. *How much do you think a writer needs to live on?*

Slightly more than most people. He, apparently, needs to drink more alcohol. He also needs to travel. Most people are not Fernando Pessoa or Philip Larkin. You need to go to other places for that imaginative push which may or may not turn into something purposeful. It is not, God help us, that you are going to write an account of the journey, complete with descriptions of who got in and out of the carriage. It is more the matter of being absent. It's not cheap to go to India, Russia or Peru, although it's probably cheaper than going from London to the Lake District on a 'Virgin' train.

A precise sum would be £X + 52A + 2RT, where X is the same as anyone else needs, A is the cost of the weekly alcoholic supplement and RT is the price of a return air ticket.

2. *Do you think a serious writer can earn this sum by his writing, and if so, how?*

The general rule is that the sales of a book are in inverse proportion to its merit. Look at the bestseller lists. But there are exceptions. All classics sell well. Some very good books sell well. The problem is with good books – the work of the average 'serious writer' – most of which don't sell at all. The literary agent George Greenfield reckoned there were 300 novelists in Britain today making more than £50,000 a year. I would think that a very generous estimate, and that less than a third of those are 'serious'.

So, the short answer is No. The exceptions are too few to threaten the rule.

3. *If not, what do you think is the most suitable second occupation for him?*

To have an earning spouse or partner and no children. Failing that, a job with low energy demands and long holidays. Teaching in a school is too draining, but I should think lecturing in a college would be a possibility, provided it doesn't drag you into writing intertextual campus blockbusters. Henry Green worked satisfactorily in the family business making lavatory seats, but few such openings exist today.

Journalism on the staff of a newspaper helps you travel, ask questions and learn things, but it's hard to make enough money from it.

A writer called Jeremy Brooks advised me to be a night porter in a hotel. By day you would sleep or hang out in Soho pubs; by night you worked on your novel, undisturbed except for the odd latecomer. This is a job that suits you when you are 23, but could become tedious.

4. *Do you think literature suffers from the diversion of a writer's energy into other employments or is enriched by it?*

Enriched. Anything that stops novelists writing about their neighbours and themselves in thin and instantly penetrable disguise is a good thing.

5. *Do you think the State or any other institution should do more for writers?*

In theory, no. Writers are entitled to the same state benefits as anyone else and I have never been convinced that their art responds to further payments. However, the Arts Council could try a system of grants like those administered by the Society of Authors, in which people submit outlines of work for which they have publishing contracts and a further gift from the Society buys them time.

I also think the State could help publishers. First books are notoriously hard to get accepted and they don't make any money. Yet if they cannot get their work into print, many writers give up. They cannot go on believing in themselves when no one else does. So I would like to see a programme that helped finance the publication of first books.

However, this would be tricky to administer because the problem is that most publishers already bring out far too much. Quality is the key. It could be almost like an EC agricultural policy. Every modest grant to bring out a promising first timer might be contingent on a set-aside agreement not to publish half a dozen titles of known rubbish.

This scheme, as you can see, still needs refining.

6. *Are you satisfied with your own solution of the problem and have you any specific advice to give to young people who wish to earn their living by writing?*

I have no solution, only a constantly changing arrangement.

My advice would be: Don't expect to make a living from writing, and don't take the disastrous step of trying to write for what you suppose is a 'market'. Be uncompromising in what you write. Do only your best. Think *Grimus*.

SEBASTIAN FAULKS *is the author of four novels, including* The Girl at the Lion D'Or *and* Birdsong, *and one work of non-fiction,* The Fatal Englishman. *His new novel,* Charlotte Gray, *will be published in September 1998.*

Margaret Forster

1. *How much do you think a writer needs to live on?*

This is such an impossible question I can't believe it was ever phrased like this – it's tedious to try to take it seriously. Tell me whether this writer lives alone or not, tell me who depends on the writer, tell me where the writer lives – then I might bother.

2. *Do you think a serious writer can earn this sum by his writing, and if so, how?*

No serious writers, starting off, can possibly earn enough to support their life styles unless they literally exist in a hut on bread and water – but why should that be so awful? Why should they expect their writing immediately to earn them a living? It isn't as though they've served apprenticeships as electricians or plumbers, or qualified as doctors or barristers, and therefore could reasonably expect to do so. There is no training to be a writer which can automatically claim remuneration.

3. *If not, what do you think is the most suitable second occupation for him?*

Any occupation is suitable for a writer. The theory that physical exhaustion in some jobs would prevent writing is such a tempting one but impossible to prove – in fact, there's enough proof the other way to dismiss it. What people don't realise is that writing can give energy, not take it. Probably a mistake to quote my own feeble experience, but I remember very well sitting down to write feeling completely exhausted, absolutely shattered by the normal day with three children, and knowing I'd get no more than four or five broken hours of sleep at night, and in a kind of zombie-like state, convinced I was too tired even to lift my pen – and then writing, and after an hour feeling not worse but better, much better, suddenly all fresh again.

4. *Do you think literature suffers from the diversion of a writer's energy into other employments or is enriched by it?*

Again, it's a question of what kind of energy. A job uses one sort, writing another, and they can be complementary. Also, a writer can train her/himself to write in what might seem absurdly short snatches of time. Having no job and all day to write seems to me a recipe for disaster – there has to be stimulation, there has to be a great hunger to get to the writing.

5. *Do you think the State or any other institution should do more for writers?*

No. And again no, no, no. I am against all State grants to writers when they are starting off. The only case to be made for State patronage is, perhaps, the giving of some kind of pensions to writers who have done good work but never earned much from their writing and have fallen on hard times. Then, I think, a grateful State should step in, on a scale not possible for the existing Royal Society of Literature fund.

6. *Are you satisfied with your own solution of the problem and have you any specific advice to give to young people who wish to earn their living by writing?*

I was lucky. I never had to find a solution to the problem of money, and I never forget that. But I did have to find a solution to the problem of time. It's always been too easy to say that a woman at home who is 'only' a housewife and mother faces no obstacles to writing if she wants, but all women in such a common situation know how hard it is to find even an hour when children are young and there is no help, no nannies or au pairs or cleaners. What made me find that hour was the sheer desire to write – it was my thrill, my excitement, my true love. I just adored doing it, and so I managed, even if what I produced wasn't then much good. It seems to me that if that desire and love are not there, there's not much point in doing it. I hate writers who moan on about the agony and loneliness of writing – oh for God's sake, if you're so bloody agonised then don't do it. No young person should wish to write to earn their living – they have to know writing is something in them that can't *not* be done whether it earns them a living or not. It's a privilege to be a writer, it's a gift, and it's arrogant to assume a living goes with it.

MARGARET FORSTER *is the author of sixteen novels – including* Mother Can You Hear Me?, Georgy Girl, The Battle for Christabel *and* Shadow Baby *– and five works of non-fiction, among them a biography of Daphne du Maurier and a memoir of her family,* Hidden Lives. Precious Lives, *her second volume of family memoirs, will be published in September 1998.*

Victoria Glendinning

1. *How much do you think a writer needs to live on?*

A writer needs no more and no less to live on than a non-writer. It all depends on the person's tastes, expectations and responsibilities. Writers are like everyone else. We could all exist on very little indeed, but would prefer not to.

2. *Do you think a serious writer can earn this sum by his writing, and if so, how?*

I don't know what 'serious' means here. It may mean for minority or scholarly tastes, i.e. not expecting to sell many copies. Naturally that can't make much money. But some 'serious' in the sense of 'literary' writers make quite a lot of money. How, you ask? By writing books that are well supported by their publishers, and well received critically. Most of the 'serious' books that do well are simply good books. Some are not, but become fashionable, or are ephemerally entertaining, or catch the public imagination for one reason or another. Nothing wrong with that.

3. *If not, what do you think is the most suitable second occupation for him?*

If a writer's books are not making the money necessary to live on, then a job as different from writing as possible is the ideal option. To be in the 'real world' in an ordinary job feeds originality and releases the imagination better than working in a para-literary field.

For all that, many writers earn what they need by journalism, broadcasting, editing or teaching. It's not the best option, it's the easiest and probably the most natural one. It has the dubious advantage of getting one's name known by one's peers – people in the same narrow, over-cultivated field, often aspiring writers themselves.

4. *Do you think literature suffers from the diversion of a writer's energy into other employments or is enriched by it?*

It depends how much energy you have to start with. This is the most important single thing to know about yourself. Some writers find their work enlivened and sharpened by coming to it fresh from other activities. Others have to concentrate only on their work if they are to produce anything good; other commitments exhaust and dissipate their energies.

5. *Do you think the State or any other institution should do more for writers?*

I don't think the state owes any reasonably sane and able-bodied person a living, whether a writer or not. But it has to be agreed by all reasonable people a) that being a writer is at best an unstable and unreliable way of earning a living, b) that there will necessarily be fallow and unproductive periods, and c) that the national life would be unspeakably impoverished without books. I should like us to follow in some form the Irish pattern: no income tax on writers' advances or royalties.

What is wrong at the moment is the massive differentials in authors' advances. Less established writers are paid too little, successful writers are paid too much. Sanity could only be restored if publishers got together and agreed on ceilings, thus releasing funds to commission, publish and publicise worthwhile books which at the moment fall through the floorboards. This will not happen unless the market collapses, because top authors are too greedy, and publishers too competitive for the top authors, often paying them advances that can never be earned out. But top authors, if they did without 'trophy' advances, would still do well through royalties. The difference would be that they would have earned the money.

A reconstruction of the tax position, and of the publishing industry, would do far more for authors than individual prizes, grants and awards, which are of their nature arbitrary and affect very few people. If there is to be institutionalised subsidy, let it be to publishers who are prepared to have what they do with the money strictly monitored, the funds ring-fenced for new, or unusual, or uncommercial books.

6. *Are you satisfied with your own solution of the problem and have you any specific advice to give to young people who wish to earn their living by writing?*

Of course I'm not satisfied with my own solution of the problem. I muddle through. I have been self-supporting through writing for twenty years, and have benefited by just hanging in there. As in any profession, you acquire a sort of clientele and the 'goodwill' that goes with long trading. But there is no security. Write a bad or unsuccessful book, and it's over in the morning, and you have to pick yourself up and start all over again.

To a young writer starting out, I would say 'know thyself'. Do you like doing just one thing (writing), or do you like doing lots of different things? What is your energy level, and is your drive to write constant or intermittent? Will you be content to be poor for quite a long time, or do you want a lot, and want it now? That will determine not only whether you take a day-job, but the sort of books that you might write. Decisions have consequences. It's no good being self-indulgent or highfalutin' about writing, unless you have private money. Being a writer is lonely, risky and TOUGH. Don't let that stop you, though.

VICTORIA GLENDINNING *is a biographer whose subjects have included Edith Sitwell, Vita Sackville-West, Rebecca West and Anthony Trollope.*

Twice winner of the Whitbread Prize for Biography, she is also the author of two novels, The Grown Ups *and* Electricity. *Her biography of Jonathan Swift will be published in September 1998.*

Linda Grant

1. *How much do you think a writer needs to live on?*

When I was a teenager in the provinces in the 1960s and literary life was as close as the moon, I thought that if you had written even one book, some government ministry then paid you a monthly stipend to continue writing for the rest of your life. And you got royalties on top of that. Advances? I'd never heard of them. I assumed that writing was the very best job in the world and so had to be rewarded handsomely by a grateful society. What a little ignoramus. The amount I envisaged would, in today's terms, be around £50,000 a year, roughly commensurate with the salary of an editorial director of a good-sized publishing firm, because you couldn't possibly be paid less than the drones who serviced your Great Creative Gift. I still think fifty grand is about right. Some writers seem able or at least prepared to live on £6,000 a year but I don't suppose many of them have families to support or live in London. And you have to live in the capital, otherwise the books-pages people don't owe you any favours and so don't review your books. £50,000 covers the cost of London mortgages, council tax and the enormous sums you have to put by for pensions, critical illness coverage and the other kinds of insurance you need simply to live without the terror of penury in sickness and old age. Which starts, of course, at 40, authors older than that being publishers' poison.

2. *Do you think a serious writer can earn this sum by his writing, and if so, how?*

I don't know, I wish I did.

3. *If not, what do you think is the most suitable second occupation for him?*

I was a journalist before I began to write books and continue to be one because books alone don't pay me enough. I've often noted that journalism is much looked down on by those who think of themselves as 'proper' writers, and, if permissible at all, can only extend to the reviewing of books or perhaps exercising an opinion in a column. Dismissed as hackery is the kind of journalism I do which gets you out of your house and into other people's, especially if it involves spending many hours hunched over a tape recorder while the person opposite spills their guts, telling you the most intimate secrets of their lives while you observe their body language. And then you go home and transcribe the tape, listening once more for the nuance in the voice, the things unsaid. No preparation for novel-writing, that, apparently.

4. *Do you think literature suffers from the diversion of a writer's energy into other employments or is enriched by it?*

The difficulty with interspersing feature writing with the production of literary fiction or non-fiction is that the two use different parts of the brain. Literary writing isn't a busy, workaholic activity. It needs so much undistracted day-dreaming. The other difficulty with journalism is that it corrodes the style. Even at its best it is only a craft because it's driven by a demand for information and if a newspaper can't provide that, why bother reading it? Even the weekly dispensing of opinions in columns is corrosive because it trains the mind into didacticism.

5. *Do you think the State or any other institution should do more for writers?*

If there is any public money going for literature I'd rather see it spent on the budgets of public libraries to modernise their ancient stock.

6. *Are you satisfied with your own solution of the problem and have you any specific advice to give to young people who wish to earn their living by writing?*

No, I am not satisfied. I want my last novel to be made into a 'major motion picture' (with choice of director and casting given to me) and be paid a small fortune for the rights. That would be my ideal solution. My advice to a young writer starting out is to be Irish. You will be part of a great literary tradition, be in fashion, be able to sell to the large Irish-American market in the US and avoid income tax at home.

LINDA GRANT'S *first novel,* The Cast Iron Shore, *won the David Higham Award in 1996. A regular columnist and feature writer for the* Guardian, *she is also the author of two works of non-fiction,* Sexing the Millennium, *and* Remind Me Who I Am, Again, *which is due for publication in June 1998.*

Alasdair Gray

1. *How much do you think a writer needs to live on?*

As much as anyone else. Without enough food and warmth writers also die. What they need to live and write varies. Milton and Virginia Woolf needed much more (being used to it) than Jean Rhys and Knut Hamsun. (Compare *A Room of One's Own* with *Hunger*.)

2. *Do you think a serious writer can earn this sum by his writing, and if so, how?*

I have not mentioned a sum and you give me no example of a serious writer, so I will answer personally. £19,549 was my net income for the tax year 1996–97. For the past ten or twelve years I have lived comfortably on similar sums, by selling books to publishers. I am sixty-three years old and for the first fifty lived on much less.

3. *If not, what do you think is the most suitable second occupation for him?*

The work that best supports them without preventing writing. Good writers have been seamen, excise officers, housekeepers, priests, teachers, journalists, doctors, bank clerks, publishers. A few labourers and aristocrats also wrote well (Burns, Clare, Byron, Shelley) but we are mostly maintained by a lowly profession or trade. Prostitution (renting your mind or body to people who don't respect it) should be avoided when possible.

4. *Do you think literature suffers from the diversion of a writer's energy into other employments or is enriched by it?*

Diverse employments in youth are a writer's material, but protection from them is needed later.

5. *Do you think the State or any other institution should do more for writers?*

The State's main job should be spreading the national income more evenly. If it did, writers would benefit along with other lower-middle-class self-employed folk.

6. *Are you satisfied with your own solution of the problem and have you any specific advice to give to young people who wish to earn their living by writing?*

I'm doing fine. My advice to the young is: get hold of a house with more rooms than you need and sublet to lodgers. This will provide a small income, if you learn to collect it, while teaching you a lot about yourself and others.

ALASDAIR GRAY *is the author of six novels – including* Lanark: a Life in Four Books *and* 1982 Janine *– as well as two books of short stories and a collection of verse,* Old Negatives. *He is also the author of the polemic,* Why Scots Should Rule Scotland.

Romesh Gunesekera

1. *How much do you think a writer needs to live on?*

I can't improve on the 1946 answer: 'as much as anyone else.'
Except perhaps to say that maybe the real need is for other people
to have money, a regularly disposable income, a thirst for fiction
and access to a good bookshop.

2. *Do you think a serious writer can earn this sum by his writing, and if
so, how?*

Whatever the sum is, only a few will be lucky.

3. *If not, what do you think is the most suitable second occupation for him?*

I cannot generalise about suitable occupations for writers. Each
individual has to discover, by trial and error, those things that
apparently help them write and learn to avoid those things that
seem to prevent the right words from forming. These will vary from
person to person, and from time to time.

4. *Do you think literature suffers from the diversion of a writer's energy into
other employments or is enriched by it?*

A writer is a writer only when he or she is writing and at those
moments there is no diversion. The rest of the time is spent being a
writer's assistant when anything can happen.

5. *Do you think the State or any other institution should do more for writers?*

The State in its administrative capacity could make life easier for most people, including writers, by simplifying the systems we all live by. In the longer term the best it could do for writers is to ensure literacy and a decent quality of life for all its people so that reading remains a viable option.

Meanwhile, given the unpredictability of the results that flow from any writing, the more sources of support there are for writers, the better.

6. *Are you satisfied with your own solution of the problem and have you any specific advice to give to young people who wish to earn their living by writing?*

I have no solutions, only experiments. Each book I have written has had to find its own way and each one has helped to shift the balance in favour of the next.

As for advice, all I can say is that the writing I value most comes from an impulse to write because language is recognised as somehow necessary for life. With luck, that writing might also provide a living for its author, but for the writing to live it has to be an imagination's lifeline.

ROMESH GUNESEKERA *was born in Sri Lanka in 1954 and moved to London in 1972. His short story collection,* Monkfish Moon, *was published in 1992 and his first novel,* Reef, *was shortlisted for the Booker Prize in 1994. His second novel,* The Sandglass, *was published in February 1998.*

Michael Holroyd

1. How much do you think a writer needs to live on?

When Elizabeth Bowen was asked this question in 1946, she replied: 'I should like to have £3,500 a year net' – which is equivalent to more than £70,000 in 1998. I have no quarrel with that, indeed I prefer it to the £1,000 suggested by George Orwell and Stephen Spender. Of course, precisely how much writers can comfortably get by on depends on individual circumstances and temperament, but the general rule, now as then, must be that they need all they can lay their hands on while continuing to write what they want to write, and not necessarily what others want them to write. Money relieves anxiety which, like a hole in a bucket, allows creative vitality to leak away. With too little money, too much anxiety, writers come out with all sorts of nonsense. 'No man but a blockhead ever wrote except for money,' said Dr Johnson, a remark that, in the words of one of his biographers, 'has been repeated by every fatuous blockhead since his time.' But we need to remind ourselves that Johnson was arrested for debt in the very year his great dictionary was published and after many years of labour. 'Slow rises worth by poverty depressed.'

Of course it is very agreeable to be paid well, partly because it suggests that people value our work. Some money is worth more than other money. For example, the income from Public Lending Rights – the payment for the use of our books in libraries – though meagre in cash is important for morale. Far from perpetually 'chattering' as some journalists like to imagine, serious writers of books inevitably spend much of their time silent and alone – and would not have it otherwise. The money that comes with their publishers' royalty statements and Public Lending Rights notifications is evidence of an audience of readers they seldom actually meet.

2. *Do you think a serious writer can earn this sum by his writing, and if so, how?*

I guess there are perhaps a couple of dozen serious writers in Britain who can earn everything they need from their books. It depends a little on luck – the good fortune of a film adaptation or, in a broader sense, of being in fashion for a spell, or catching for a time the spirit of the age. You can engineer some luck for yourself. You can get a good agent and a good editor. You can apply for some of the fellowships, grants, bursaries and awards that Book Trust publish to help you on your way.

Newspapers report whatever is exceptional: the spectacular film of the book, the amazing advance, so the public probably receives a false picture of authors' incomes. Anyone who has judged the Arts Council Award applications (as I am doing this year) and seen the details of income and expenditure that applicants submit; anyone who has sat on the panel of judges for the Authors' Foundation and looked at the contracts between authors and publishers; anyone who has served on the Royal Literary Fund will be familiar with the endemic poverty of serious writers and will know the horrifying financial risks they take when writing books.

3. *If not, what do you think is the most suitable second occupation for him?*

Many writers find it possible to take part-time work in the world of books: editing or reviewing for the literary pages of magazines and newspapers, working in libraries, reading for publishers, teaching and so on. Other writers recommend jobs unconnected with writing, pointing out that Fielding was a police magistrate, Trollope a post office official. Spinoza apparently favoured lens-polishing; Herbert Read looked kindly on some light engineering in the afternoons. Melville, of course, took to whaling; and Joyce Cary worked in the Civil Service. Both used their experiences in their work. They are exceptional cases, but then so are we all. Knowing how useless advice is, I might as well advise writers to acquire wealthy and generous parents, or a legacy or, better still, a private income. I would certainly recommend that.

4. *Do you think literature suffers from the diversion of a writer's energy into other employments or is enriched by it?*

Serious writing is a full-time job. We do not expect scientists or lawyers or industrialists to take on other work – in fact only Members of Parliament seek other concurrent employment. They do this, they tell us, not for the money but to gain information. My view is that, except possibly for a few sequestered academic writers, we have a perfectly good grasp of the world. We know about love and death, passion and grief, simply by being alive. We read about the past, inhabit the present, speculate about the future. Writers tend to have fertile imaginations and the gift of insight. If they want to trawl for specific information they will go out and collect it, experience it, convert it into knowledge, and use that knowledge to enrich their work. All this is part of the writing process – it does not depend, for heaven's sake, on being employed not writing.

5. *Do you think the State or any other institution should do more for writers?*

We all know that literature has always needed patronage and that the patron of Shakespeare's day has given way to commercial sponsorship and State subsidy. But commercial sponsorship requires a degree of advertisement and is more attracted to performance art than the composing arts – indeed the former is often called 'live art', which leaves literature somewhat buried. There is of course room for a few big prizes – the Booker (on whose management committee I served for seven years), the Whitbread (which I once judged) and the British Literature Prize (which I twice chaired). But though I have supported these prizes I do not believe that they provide the best support for literature, which does not lend itself to judgment by democratic voting or examination marks or the simple reckoning of races and jumps. Besides, prizes create more losers than winners and in the perspective of time are generally seen as whimsical. At best, they are the icing on the cake, and we first need to make the cake itself.

So I have come to believe that the State should do more for writers. For a start the Secretary of State who has the responsibility to preserve and promote libraries should see to it that our libraries have a great deal more money to spend on books – that really would be 'education, education, education' for us all. He should then increase the public lending right fund by at least ten times. After that, which is easy, he should consult the Society of Authors, the Writers' Guild and the Royal Literary Fund as to how best he can ensure that writers who are self-employed and have become ever more financially vulnerable since members of parliament voted themselves out of the self-employed category, can be spared the terrible insecurity that comes late in life when, with little capital, their income diminishes. Perhaps the State can simply pay the Royal Literary Fund so as to help it start a non-contributory pension scheme. Certainly it can allow, even encourage, and possibly insist that the Heritage Lottery Fund purchase on behalf of the British Library and other manuscript collections the archives of older living writers – those archives which are sometimes their main capital. Without this change of policy the literary archives of the country will vanish from the country – in fact they are already doing so (the papers of Malcolm Bradbury, David Hare, Ted Hughes and Tom Stoppard are among the latest authors' archives to have left Britain).

All the above measures would avoid any suspicion of State interference – the sinister control of theme and subject matter that is associated with the State, and the loss of the writer's freedom.

The Arts Council has not found a way of helping literature to anything like the same extent as the other arts. Seats for opera, dance, concerts and the theatre are subsidised; book prices are not. One reason for this is a belief that the performing arts are far more expensive to produce than the composing arts, painting and literature. It is sometimes forgotten that a single book needs paper-makers, printers, binders, publishers, booksellers, all with their employees and offices – not to forget the author in his garret. It is now a matter of urgency that the Arts Council, to employ one of its own favourite phrases, make the playing field more level without taking money away from the other art forms. In other words, it must get more from the government.

Finally, a plea. Let us stop using the cliché 'tax payers' money'. It is an inaccurate phrase pumped out by all governments when they do not want to shell out a bloody penny. Tax payers' money is actually the money tax payers keep after paying whatever is legitimately due to the government in tax. What the Arts Council needs for literature is more central government funding – money that will not be lost, but will circulate in the community and nourish its novelists, poets and, of course, biographers.

6. *Are you satisfied with your own solution of the problem and have you any specific advice to give to young people who wish to earn their living by writing?*

I have been far more successful in finding a solution to my financial problems than I thought possible at the beginning. For my first book, a biography of Hugh Kingsmill, I received an advance of £25 – more of a retreat, as Kingsmill himself would have said, than an advance. I used up my savings, bullied my parents and even grandparents into giving me a little money, took odd jobs, and somehow got through. For *Lytton Strachey* my advance shot up 100% to £50. I got two fellowships from the United States and two grants in Britain, began writing literary journalism, renegotiated my contract as many times as Britain has renegotiated her place in

Europe, and somehow got through again. For *Augustus John*, I got an advance of £4,000 in Britain and $40,000 in the United States – I was beginning to become financially respectable. My advance in 1987 for *Bernard Shaw*, the only one to attract the attention of the newspapers (one of them described it as 'obscene'), was £625,000. However this was not the lottery bonanza it was reported to be. It was payment over twelve years for five volumes in hardback and paperback – in other words, it was a middle-age pension that was to free me from literary journalism. It has worked out at between £40,000 and £50,000 a year gross – not quite in the Elizabeth Bowen category, but not too far off. By the time I receive the final payment, the advance for my next book, the mysterious *Basil Street Blues*, will begin.

My advice to anyone wishing to be an author is: Don't. But if you must, then don't send your manuscript to me. Why should I help what may be a talented rival into an already overcrowded market place? What we need are more readers, not more authors. Nevertheless I would advise any writer to join the Society of Authors as soon as possible; to use the local library; to find out about Arvon courses; to buy the *Writers' & Artists' Yearbook;* and never to read aloud his or her work-in-progress to friends.

Finally I repeat my initial warning: Don't. The predicament of contemporary literature finds an unhappy symbol in the plight of the Royal Society of Literature, which may be without a headquarters before the end of the year.

MICHAEL HOLROYD *is the author of a number of biographies, including* Lytton Strachey, Augustus John *and* Bernard Shaw. *A past Chairman of the Society of Authors and past President of English PEN, he was awarded the CBE in 1989 for services to literature.*

Michael Ignatieff

1. *How much do you think a writer needs to live on?*

It depends on the number of his dependents. If he has few, he needs little. If he has few, however, he may have little to write about.

2. *Do you think a serious writer can earn this sum by his writing, and if so, how?*

It depends on how many pots a writer can keep simmering on his stove at any one time.

3. *If not, what do you think is the most suitable second occupation for him?*

Something that has nothing to do with writing. Kafka dreamed of being a waiter at a beach-front restaurant in Tel Aviv. Wallace Stevens sold life insurance. Dag Hammarskjöld was Secretary General of the United Nations.

4. *Do you think literature suffers from the diversion of a writer's energy into other employments or is enriched by it?*

A distant relative of mine – then the editor of a newspaper – once asked Tolstoy for a contribution and was told, in reply, that journalism was a brothel which it was easy to enter but impossible to escape.

5. *Do you think the State or any other institution should do more for writers?*

The state should leave writers alone.

6. *Are you satisfied with your own solution of the problem and have you any specific advice to give to young people who wish to earn their living by writing?*

I would be entirely satisfied with my solution if I could get away with doing less work. As for the rest, all advice, especially to 'young people', is useless.

MICHAEL IGNATIEFF *is a writer, historian, academic and broadcaster. Since 1984, he has worked as a freelance writer, presenting television programmes for the BBC, scripting television plays, feature films, novels and works of non-fiction. Between 1989 and 1993 he was the host of BBC 2's* The Late Show. *His book of essays,* The Warrior's Honour, *was published in February 1998.*

A. L. Kennedy

1. *How much do you think a writer needs to live on?*

A writer needs only as much as anyone else to live on. If he or she is self-employed, then obviously some work-related expenses are tax-deductible. She or he may choose to be responsible or irresponsible with regard to tax and national insurance, employing an accountant and so forth, much as any other person may. Additional, non-deductible expenses might include eye-catching frocks, designer jackets, cocaine and alcohol, but these would tend to arise amongst writers who are already relatively financially comfortable. The pace of life a young writer may be drawn into, particularly having made a move to London (although I wouldn't argue such a move was still necessary) can be beguiling but ruinous – to say nothing of addictively bad for the health.

But, frankly, in a country with no minimum wage and an appalling percentage of the population unable to buy adequate food, the – sometimes self-inflicted – financial gripes of writers wouldn't be my first concern.

2. *Do you think a serious writer can earn this sum by his writing, and if so, how?*

A 'serious' writer – and I take that to be as loose a term as it seems – would have great difficulty earning a modest living only by writing 'seriously'. Women authors also seem to be in a slightly weaker position here. A male writer may well have a wife who works to support the demands of his delicately palpitating brain. In our current society, it's still less usual for the reverse to happen.

Of course, a 'serious' writer can earn an adequate or more-than-adequate income by also writing not 'seriously'. So in will creep journalism, reviewing, writing for film and television, pornography under assumed names, advertising copy and all the other common options offered to a pen for hire.

Although publishers will always encourage writers to give up their day job, devote themselves utterly to their work, to make the emotional commitment to perfecting their craft that this implies, and to generally come up with books in a clearer atmosphere, the unspoken agreement is that writers will, in fact, subsidise low advances from publishers by doing other work. This is particularly true at the beginning of a writer's career, when the relatively large number of awards open to young authors can be all that ever manages to buy them time to actually produce the second or third book.

Obviously, aggressive agenting, beauty contests held with competitive bidding for books that don't exist and regular hype gold rushes also don't help either writers, or publishers, or indeed agents, in the long run. I can, however, understand the impatience and insecurity that would lead to demands for criminally unrealistic advances for any individuals who can get away with them. Sadly, these tend either to place unknown authors under impossible pressure, or to gold-plate already well-established names.

3. *If not, what do you think is the most suitable second occupation for him?*

I have no idea. Different temperaments respond better to different environments and stimuli. Given the limited abilities of many writers in areas other than the imaginative, the possibilities for most – myself included – are less than numberless and often depressing. I, for example, sold double glazing and brushes in an attempt to ease my way when first writing. The other, sometimes ghastly option would involve teaching writing when you yourself are still learning how. As less and less money goes into community education and social work departments, options here are decreasing.

Once again, I would have to point out that a great many people in Britain do not even have the opportunity to train for the job they feel they would be most suited to, never mind securing it.

4. *Do you think literature suffers from the diversion of a writer's energy into other employments or is enriched by it?*

Probably, on balance, literature suffers when authors burn out, overly stressed by the demands of two or more occupations. Extreme tiredness can produce inarticulacy and long-term overwork can produce illness – a serious problem for someone who is self-employed and may have few savings. Pressures to accommodate long hours spent writing and, perhaps, another, additional job and the increasing amount of travelling that authors are expected to do in order to promote their books can all leave writers' personal lives in complicated shreds. Writers, working at home, may well be expected to perform domestic chores and child care, in addition to pursuing their calling. Obviously, this usually impacts on female writers more than on male writers.

It is good if writing is not always carried out in a rarefied atmosphere, but the silencing of all but our nation's strongest and already most often represented voices by economic pressures is our loss. Middle-class, London-based, English, male writers are still most likely to have the easiest time getting into print.

5. *Do you think the State or any other institution should do more for writers?*

The State should have a coherent arts policy which acknowledges the importance of the arts as an employer, as an index and guardian of our national well-being and as a source of communal and individual joy, encouragement and enlightenment. This might lead to the support of writers, as indeed it might interact with a sane and humane education policy. We have neither, and neither is likely to develop in the current climate where the basic human rights of all but our most able citizens are being eroded on a daily basis. First support the schools and the hospitals adequately, then look to employment, including the arts.

6. *Are you satisfied with your own solution of the problem and have you any specific advice to give to young people who wish to earn their living by writing?*

I am not satisfied with my own solution to the problems of earning a living by writing. I am trapped in a cycle of working in order to earn money in order to buy time in order to do the work I want to. I never write anything I wouldn't wish to, but I frequently do write when I don't wish to. I am heartily tired of subsisting in a blur of attenuated friendships, postponements of pleasure and insanely pressured relationships. I have unwittingly decided to pay too high a price for the undoubted joy that writing brings me. I am, however, grateful for any kind of employment, for a good deal of material comfort, for a job involving few industrial injuries or dangers and for the patience of those I love. I wouldn't presume to advise anyone to write or not write. In my experience, if someone truly wants to write, they will. Having made the decision to write, they owe their craft all the application they can give – it will only prosper from a genuine commitment. They also owe themselves as much protection against stress, exploitation and despair as they can arrange.

A. L. KENNEDY *is the author of three collections of short stories, two novels and a work of non-fiction, as well as a number of plays and screenplays. Her writing has won many awards, including the Scottish Arts Council Book Award and the Somerset Maugham Award, and she was chosen in 1993 as one of* Granta *magazine's Best of Young British Novelists. Her most recent collection of short stories,* Original Bliss, *was published in 1997.*

Hanif Kureishi

1. *How much do you think a writer needs to live on?*

Writers require different amounts of money at different periods of their life. When I began to write seriously, not long after I left university, I was on the dole, and supported by my girlfriend. For about five years I wrote plays which were performed in various fringe theatres, and later at the Royal Court and by the Royal Shakespeare Company. (All these theatres were, incidentally, supported by the Arts Council.) I got by; but I didn't make any significant money – and nor did I need any – until I wrote my first film, *My Beautiful Launderette*. This, followed by *Sammy and Rosie Get Laid*, enabled me to buy the time – about two years – to write my first novel, *The Buddha of Suburbia*. After that my earnings went up, but so did my outgoings.

In the end, what writers must do is spend less than they earn. Nevertheless, they will probably never have financial security in the way that a doctor, lawyer or businessman might. Most writers have little idea how much they will earn in the next couple of years, and will rarely have any idea of what their financial situation will be in five years time. They may have written a successful novel, contracted writer's block, or been sacked by their publisher. For five years I was put on a wage by my publishers, Faber and Faber, and this made me feel more secure. On the other hand a little financial insecurity won't harm a writer; it might make her work harder. What most writers need more than anything, apart from inspiration, is time and that is an expensive commodity.

2. *Do you think a serious writer can earn this sum by his writing, and if so, how?*

It is probably easier now for writers to earn a living than in the past. Most novels seem to end up on either the big or small screen, and many novelists do adaptations of other writers' novels. The expansion of the media has provided opportunities for writers, though it won't necessarily help improve the quality of their work.

3. *If not, what do you think is the most suitable second occupation for him?*

Writing is a business as well as an art. Most writers spend a lot of time talking to agents, publishers, journalists, translators, film producers, as well as supervising the publication of their work in various countries and languages. Most working writers these days are also encouraged to do a lot of publicity, which is often enervating and boring. Reading tours too, can take up a lot of time. Unfortunately, it has become part of the process of selling books. The most suitable occupation for a writer is writing. Most of the working writers that I know actually write most of the day. This is both a necessity, and – fortunately for the writers – something they like to do. It is an absorbing profession, which becomes more interesting as one gets older. Some writers do other things, like reviewing and travel writing, but none of it can provide the satisfactions of a runaway imagination.

4. *Do you think literature suffers from the diversion of a writer's energy into other employments or is enriched by it?*

Good writers can draw strength and inspiration from whatever they do. But other forms of writing, and journalism in particular, which requires no use of the imagination, can be stifling and tiring.

5. *Do you think the State or any other institution should do more for writers?*

There are literary activities which could, usefully, be sponsored by the state. I would like to believe that there are dozens of books in foreign languages that could be usefully translated into English, to broaden our sense of the world and our understanding of what other writers are doing. Those of us who are fortunate enough to write in English should be aware of interesting and innovative writers whose language is less accessible. I think it would enrich our literary culture for the state to sponsor a certain amount of this. However, the best thing the state could do for literature – and for writers – is provide a comprehensive, accessible, properly-funded library service.

6. *Are you satisfied with your own solution of the problem and have you any specific advice to give to young people who wish to earn their living by writing?*

I have never wanted to do anything else but write for a living. When I started out I never considered the material aspect; it just seemed impossible that I would do anything else. I am aware now that what I do is a great privilege, and I can also see how hard it is to make a decent, sustained living by writing. It is difficult to be prescriptive about how anyone else might do it, because writers have such different talents. Some writers love writing for film, while others would consider it a betrayal; some writers see television as the National Theatre of our time, and others see it as rubbish. Just as every writer has to find her own style or voice, every writer probably has to find their own financial way.

Playwright, scriptwriter and novelist, HANIF KUREISHI's *first film,* My Beautiful Launderette, *was released in 1986. The author of three novels –* The Buddha of Suburbia, The Black Album *and the newly published* Intimacy *– he has also published a book of short stories,* Love in a Blue Time, *and co-edited* The Faber Book of Pop *with Jon Savage.*

Toby Litt

1. *How much do you think a writer needs to live on?*

I live in London. I need around £20,000 a year to live on. If I lived somewhere else, I'd need less. If I had children or a drug habit (or both), I'd need more.

2. *Do you think a serious writer can earn this sum by his writing, and if so, how?*

It is only since signing a screenwriting contract that I have been able to give up my day job.

The advance I received for my first two books was well above average. But, even so, unless I had gone to live somewhere very cheap, it wouldn't have lasted me more than a year.

And each of these two books took a year to write.

3. *If not, what do you think is the most suitable second occupation for him?*

Before I was able to go full-time as a writer I taught English in Prague, worked in Fielder's Bookshop, Wimbledon, and subtitled for ITV and Channel 5.

With understanding bosses, unconventional hours, and a massively supportive girlfriend, I was just about able to write (evenings, days off, weekends, holidays) whilst holding down these jobs.

What I most disliked during the two years I spent working as a bookseller was that one bad (i.e. aggressive, malicious, chippy) customer could ruin my entire day.

I would get home in the evening, fizzing with suppressed anger – anger that the job itself gave me no means of expressing. I would either start writing whilst still angry or try to calm down by having a drink. But, after having a drink, I would become a lot less likely to work; and, if still angry, I was more inclined to write aggressively (that is *against* my imagined readers) than affably (*for* them). I have never found alcohol or anger anything other than harmful to my writing.

This suggests that a writer's second occupation should be relatively emotionally uninvolving.

(I should add that bookselling taught me a great deal about – among other things – how and why people read what they read.)

Whilst working as a subtitler, I spent around eight hours a day looking at a computer screen and typing. Once home, I had absolutely no desire to stare at another computer screen or do yet more typing. With so many jobs nowadays based around computer work, this kind of duplication is a real problem for the writer – especially one who writes on a PC.

This suggests that a writer's second occupation shouldn't too closely resemble writing.

TEFL is the job I have found most compatible with writing. This is probably because I only taught for twelve to sixteen hours a week.

Yet, apart from the hours of free time I gained, there were other clear benefits. In class I was constantly having to clarify and simplify what I was saying. My grammar and spelling improved. I got to live in a beautiful foreign city surrounded by a language not my own.

At a certain stage, all this can be invaluable.

4. *Do you think literature suffers from the diversion of a writer's energy into other employments or is enriched by it?*

I play my Fender Telecaster very loud. That helps a great deal.

5. *Do you think the State or any other institution should do more for writers?*

If the State were to directly support writers, it should be those at the end rather than the beginning of their careers. Pensions are a lot less sexy than prizes, but do a lot more good.

However, it is probably healthier for the writer to be ignored or despised by the State than beholden to it.

Whilst the only political hero I have ever had, Vaclav Havel, produced numerous important plays and essays during his years as a dissident, his writings since becoming President have been pure UN-speak – hardly less banal (it pains me to say) than the speeches of Klement Gottwald.

This – written small rather than large – is what I would fear from State patronage: dissidence being coaxed towards banality.

('The relationship between the writer and the State' is the kind of topic that makes me nostalgic for the Cold War.)

6. *Are you satisfied with your own solution of the problem and have you any specific advice to give to young people who wish to earn their living by writing?*

My criterion for giving up my day job has always been, 'I need enough money to survive for a year. Hopefully, during that year, I will be able to earn enough to make it through the next year. If not, I'll just have to go back to work.'

That is my solution.

Born in 1968, TOBY LITT *is the author of a collection of short stories,* Adventures in Capitalism, *and a novel,* Beatniks, *which was published in 1997.*

Penelope Lively

1. *How much do you think a writer needs to live on?*

An adequate sufficiency – enough for a roof over the head, food, clothing and something extra for the enrichment of the soul and spirits – which in the case of a writer means above all the possibility of buying books and of getting out and about. The sufficiency will vary according to circumstance, of course – what does for a single person won't do for a family.

2. *Do you think a serious writer can earn this sum by his writing, and if so, how?*

No. Or at least not for years and even then only for a fortunate few. So this is where the trouble starts. Incidentally, this term 'serious writer' is something of a teaser but I take it to mean one whose central concern in writing is the exploration and expression of ideas or of a particular vision of the world. This definition could well be disputed but implicit in the concept of seriousness seems to be the suggestion that it does not cater to popular taste and is therefore commercially unsound, which is very likely and is confirmed by a glance at the bestseller lists, any week: only one or two 'serious' books will surface.

3. *If not, what do you think is the most suitable second occupation for him?*

Nobody, but nobody, should assume that a living can be earned from writing (so-called 'serious' or indeed any other kind). Nor should anyone who has had a few good years assume that this will go on for ever. Every writer should have a fall-back position or be prepared to change tactics, diversify, try something entirely different – or have the good fortune of a partner in steady employment. Most start from the fall-back position – earning a living at something else and slotting in the writing when possible. Fine. Frustrating, maybe, but good training. Any writer may have to return to that. So what is a suitable occupation? Anything. I see nothing wrong with writing to order, if the order comes – journalism, for instance. Good discipline, again. Physical labour is nicely undemanding but can leave you too exhausted to apply yourself to anything else. Looking after children may be unavoidable and has the same effect. I favour the idea of some acquired trade or craft that could be done at home at convenient hours, bookbinding, say, or watch repair or picture-framing or upholstery or cabinet-making. Where grander occupations are concerned, there is a fine traditional link between writing and university teaching or librarianship.

4. *Do you think literature suffers from the diversion of a writer's energy into other employments or is enriched by it?*

Every writer needs to get involved with unfamiliar worlds – you never know from where the lightning will strike. As Henry Reed said in response to the 1946 questionnaire: '. . . think what we should miss if Melville had never gone whaling.' A spell on an oil rig may be a poor equivalent, in late twentieth-century terms, but still an opportunity to be seized and no doubt in the fullness of time it will occur to someone to set up a Writer-in-Residence scheme. But on a more mundane level, anything has potential, where the beady eye of the writer is concerned. We are a predatory lot, and need fodder. Toiling at the rock-face of clerical work, the advertising agency or the supermarket check-out may numb the mind at the time but at least you are amongst others, and other people are the writer's material (alongside yourself, of course). A solitary lifetime at the desk seems to me the ultimate danger. As is, also, an acquaintance composed entirely of other writers, who may indeed be stimulating and productive company but with whom you have too much in common. We all need the inspiration and provocation of new experience. Though, that being said, clearly a life sentence in an insurance office or the equivalent will leave no time or energy for writing. If things go reasonably well, you should be able to strike a balance – outside activities earn time for writing.

5. *Do you think the State or any other institution should do more for writers?*

Except that the economic climate may make flexibility impossible. Jobs dry up, as in the eighties, and those writers valiantly trying to diversify found that they couldn't. Then what? Then we come to the tricky question of subsidy. How much should there be? Who should get it? Who should decide who gets it? Questions to which there can be no precise answers. There is a good deal of subsidy around nowadays. Arts Council bursaries, writing fellowship and residencies, an assortment of other small bursaries, prizes and awards, especially for younger writers. But plenty never come within sniffing distance of any of these. I see no easy solution. The notion of an automatic living wage for anyone with pretensions to the title of writer appals me, though I do think that older writers of quality whose earning days are over should get some help – but there are certain resources in place for that. The writers replying to Cyril Connolly's questionnaire were for the most part aghast at the notion of state funding: 'He who pays the piper calls the tune.' They had a point – the danger, to my mind, is the tyranny of current literary fashion and the dictation of a particular climate of taste or prejudice. Bursaries and fellowships can also be susceptible to the winds of fashion. Write the expedient kind of thing and you will find a paymaster; don't, and you won't.

6. *Are you satisfied with your own solution of the problem and have you any specific advice to give to young people who wish to earn their living by writing?*

Advice to the aspiring writer. If you are hell bent on writing you will do it anyway, so take note of the points made earlier about the foolhardy nature of the enterprise, equip yourself with alternative marketable skills (or a spouse in merchant banking), get a roof over your head that will not be an on-going financial burden, think about tedious stuff like a pension scheme – even if you are twenty-one. And remember that in the world of publishing nothing is stable – fashions change, editors' heads roll, your day may very well come (and, equally, go).

My own experience has been to climb slowly up from earning next to nothing. I've been fortunate. But I have never had that Writing Fellowship on an oil rig and might be a different writer if I had.

PENELOPE LIVELY *has written many prize-winning novels and collections of short stories for both adults and children – among them* Moon Tiger, *which won the 1987 Booker Prize. As well as being a Fellow of the Royal Society of Literature, she is also a member of PEN and the Society of Authors. Her latest collection of short stories,* Beyond the Blue Mountains, *is published in June 1998.*

Shena Mackay

1. *How much do you think a writer needs to live on?*

How long is a piece of string? It is impossible to generalise. Like everyone else, a writer needs an income commensurate with his or her responsibilities and the expenses incurred by the job. There are writers, fewer now than when the original questionnaire came out, with private incomes; there are writers with comfortably-off partners or spouses, there are writers with retreats and nannies, and there are writers who have to clear a space on the kitchen table, and lone parents trying to earn enough to support their children. There are writers who become ill, and elderly, indigent writers who have devoted their lives to their art who have no resources except such help as can be offered by friends or charities such as the excellent Royal Literary Fund or those administered by the Society of Authors. Constant worry about money debilitates, diminishes and prevents artists from fulfilling their potential.

2. *Do you think a serious writer can earn this sum by his writing, and if so, how?*

In most cases, no. Certainly not by concentrating exclusively on the real work, that is the prose or poetry that she or he should be writing. It is ironic that the more successful a writer is, the more he or she will be asked to do things that take her away from that real work, and she is often not in a position to refuse. (The 1946 questionnaire was heavily biased towards the male writer so

henceforth I will use she rather than he or she). Although a
commission for a story or article can inspire or provide a platform
for an idea, much time and energy can be wasted on the 'What I Did
On My Hols' type of piece. Some writers enjoy teaching 'creative
writing' while to others the 'workshop' is anathema; in either case
the remuneration is small.

3. *If not, what do you think is the most suitable second occupation for him?*

The assumption is that writing is a middle-class occupation, although
I know of one author who is a postman and one who is a bus
conductor. Writers used to boast on their book jackets of all the
bizarre trades they had followed but most of them dreamed of giving
up the day job or, like Faulkner (who worked as a coal-heaver), the
night job. Unless a writer is trained in some other profession, the
only jobs open to her are low-paid and as everybody knows there are
few of those available. So-called unskilled jobs demand abilities that
writers might not possess. Personally, I wouldn't recommend mush-
room picking, and shop work is exhausting. The ideal secondary
occupation for a writer would be something that does not use the
same kind of energy as writing and that would not dominate her
thoughts. Teaching, therefore, would be ruled out, and reviewing,
although they are the means by which many writers live. Trollope's
Mr Booker, in *The Way We Live Now*, is a nice illustration of a reviewer
in a *quid pro quo* dilemma: 'He felt it to be hard on him that he
should be compelled, by the exigencies of his position, to descend so
low in literature; but it did not occur to him to reflect that in fact he
was not compelled, and that he was quite at liberty to break stones,
or to starve honestly, if no other more honest mode of carrying on
his career was open to him. "If I didn't, somebody else would," he
said to himself.' Another drawback to reviewing is that the reviewer
has time to read only books that are sent to her rather than, for
example, expanding her knowledge of the classics or other
literatures.

    As writing is essentially a solitary occupation, something involving other people, animals or plants would be pleasant. I should like to be a gardener in one of the hot houses at Kew. Other suggestions, providing they paid enough: a warder in a gallery or museum, a lollipop person or a catcher in the rye, some tactile physical work such as painting and decorating or ladling molten wax for a sculptor, dog-walking, rowing a ferryboat – or anything involving a different art form.

4. *Do you think literature suffers from the diversion of a writer's energy into other employments or is enriched by it?*

Too many writers end up with nothing to write about except writers, i.e. themselves, because they have never known or have lost touch with the world of work outside their own sphere. It should not be forgotten, though, that many writers, mostly women but some men, put a great deal of work into looking after their children. Cyril Connolly was wrong about the pram in the hall: having children enriches an artist immeasurably.

5. *Do you think the State or any other institution should do more for writers?*

A civilisation is judged by its art. It is a truism that the arts, including the theatre (which is dependent on writers), generate a huge revenue for this country. There should be State pensions for committed artists in all fields, regardless of success and other means by which they have supplemented their earnings. Young writers should not expect preferential treatment, but older writers should qualify for the dole when on their uppers. Private and corporate patronage, providing it has no strings attached, should be offered more often; instead of bombarding people with angst-laden adjurements to take out private pension plans and health insurance, companies might do something to promote peace of mind and a reasonable income for writers. Public Lending Right, which was fought for so hard by its supporters, does make a difference to some writers by giving them a very small amount of money for each library borrowing of their books. There are various grants and bursaries too, but a fair day's wage for a fair day's work sounds an attractive proposition.

6. *Are you satisfied with your own solution of the problem and have you any specific advice to give to young people who wish to earn their living by writing?*

No. It requires more thought and analysis. To a young person who expressed a desire to earn a living by writing I should say, 'We poets in our youth begin in gladness; but thereof comes in the end despondency and madness.' If she were a real writer and not somebody just interested in self-promotion, money and seeing her book plastered on the walls of the underground as she rode the escalator, she would look up the quotation and carry on writing in spite of anything I told her.

SHENA MACKAY *was born in Edinburgh. She is the author of two novellas, three collections of short stories and seven novels, including* Dunedin *and* The Orchard on Fire, *which was shortlisted for the 1996 Booker Prize. Her new novel,* The Artist's Widow, *will be published in July.*

Hilary Mantel

1. *How much do you think a writer needs to live on?*

In the ideal world, all published writers would be as rich as Croesus.
They could then indulge in dissipation and eccentricity on a scale
the public has a right to expect.

   Writers don't need more than anyone else. When they begin,
perhaps they should have less than anyone else; this is a spur to
ambition. However, once they have assumed the persona of 'writer',
noblesse oblige. There must be sufficient money for champagne to
cheer up friends whose work is rejected, and for postage stamps to
return unsolicited manuscripts. To engage the interest of the
Sunday papers, it is necessary to build up a big drug habit. Female
writers absolutely must not be seen to dress out of Marks & Spencer.
Also, writers who venture abroad must always travel first class and
stay at the best hotels. Otherwise, they encounter hazards and
hardships, write very dull books about them, and become a burden
to the spirit.

2. *Do you think a serious writer can earn this sum by his writing, and if
so, how?*

I am not sure I know any serious writers. I do not like to think how
they earn their living.

3. If not, what do you think is the most suitable second occupation for him?

If you cannot earn as much as you would like to have, then journalism is convenient. The danger is that you become, as Stevenson says, 'wedded to cheap finish'.

The church and the military impose self-censorship, and practice of the law destroys prose style. Medicine and social work provide plots, but also create cynicism, which in writers is a blight. Teaching erodes faith in the future, and ask yourself – has there ever been a dentist who succeeded in the word line?

Teaching creative writing might be a good idea. There is always a market for the blind leading the blind.

It is probably best to be a respectable artisan or shopkeeper. Bookselling (preferably in the second-hand market) would be a corrective to self-satisfaction.

It is useful to know people's hopes and fears, so one might become a fortune-teller. It is useful to see inside their houses, so one might become an estate agent, or daily cleaner.

The best alternative occupation would be non-verbal, and pursued outdoors – for instance, collecting supermarket trolleys from far-flung parking bays. It should ideally be a job that can be done by a person of very low intellectual attainment, so that you give your wonderful brain a rest. Do not worry that you are depriving some sad moron of employment. That sad moron will soon have tied up a multi-million book-film deal in the US, while you are dunning Messrs Quill & Blotte for the £750 you thought your Serious Writing entitled you to.

4. Do you think literature suffers from the diversion of a writer's energy into other employments or is enriched by it?

Literature never suffers; it has no nerves. It is readers who suffer. One thing that makes them suffer is novels about characters who are writing novels. For that reason, it may be good for writers to have other occupations, or at least live with people who have them.

But this question – indeed, all these questions – presuppose that writers have something in common – common needs, common temperaments. I think that is a romantic fallacy. The questions also presume that a writer feels part of, or is concerned to serve, a tradition called 'literature'.

As a working writer, I would think it a gross and paralysing presumption to concern myself with what serves the culture and what does not. Why should I serve it? I have certain skills, and I have had some luck, which has allowed me to display those skills and earn money from them. I know what I write today. I regret what I wrote yesterday. I fear what I may write tomorrow. That is all I know about the occupation. I cannot generalise from the truths of my own life or personality. I cannot make recommendations for other temperaments. I can only see myself as the sniper on the roof; I cannot say what are the best boots to be worn by those who are marching in someone else's army.

5. *Do you think the State or any other institution should do more for writers?*

In general, I do not believe that the state should be encouraged to do much more than it does now, in any sphere. I doubt it should become the patron of individual artists, except by an indirect method.

It may be that the best way for the state to help writers is to provide generous funds to public libraries. If the library service is maintained in glory, anyone can read and learn – whatever their background, however poor or philistine it may be. Free public libraries breed writers and readers of the future; this has been the case for many years, and will continue to be so now that information is a crucial and rationed commodity.

A well-resourced public library system should bring with it a well-resourced system for Public Lending Right, which is of immediate benefit to writers.

After this has been attended to, I would (if I had to dole out the funds) give the money to the Arvon Foundation, which runs writing courses which encourage new talent.

My lowest priority would be grants to individuals, or to specific writing projects. I see, of course, that for the beneficiaries these grants are very wonderful things to have.

The established, professional writer might welcome some fresh thinking about tax allowances; some very strange reliefs operate, and where there should be relief, there is none. But this is an eternal truth, of course.

6. *Are you satisfied with your own solution of the problem and have you any specific advice to give to young people who wish to earn their living by writing?*

I can't myself find an accommodation that lasts for more than six months. It's such a long time between books, so you feel you must review, or do something because you want some money, or you feel you should keep your name around, or because you simply want to finish a piece, any piece: or because you are procrastinating, knowing that your next book is not ready to be written. What I need – and I can speak only for myself – is time. And somehow you have to buy it.

If I were to advise a young writer, I would mention that this question of time is vital. You can look back – for me, over eight books, as I write – and work out the hourly rate for a novelist. It's pence per hour, not pounds. So you must decide where your ambition and self-respect resides. You will always work long and unsociable hours, and the pay-off may be long-delayed.

If you feel you could be ambitious in another trade, you should pursue it. Writing is a good trade for people who can't fit into organisations, or who have poor health, or are just a bit strange. I can't see why you'd want to do it, unless you fell into those categories.

To succeed – financially or otherwise – you must want to write more than you want anything else.

It may be protective to your sensibilities if you can believe that no one has a right to earn a living by being a writer, or any kind of artist.

If you do not believe this, you should develop a less imperious talent, and think daily about those who may be better writers than yourself, but who are thwarted by circumstance and ill-luck.

These are generalisations. The only specific advice I can give to a young writer is this: as soon as you start earning you should engage a specialist accountant, so that you are sure your affairs are well-arranged. You know what you are, but not what you may be. Who knows: you might even get rich.

HILARY MANTEL *is the author of seven novels, including* Every Day is Mother's Day, Fludd, A Place of Greater Safety, An Experiment in Love *and* Eight Months on Ghazza Street, *which is currently being made into a film. Her new novel,* The Giant, O'Brien, *will be published in September 1998.*

Adrian Mitchell

I'm sorry that I can't sit down and write you a beautiful poem on this subject but, after about 35 years as a freelance poet, playwright and novelist for adults and children, I have to work seven days a week in order to keep afloat financially.

But I enclose an article I published in the *New Statesman* in 1994. Unfortunately there was little reaction to it, especially from those to whom it was directed – notably the Arts Council.

I was assured by Gary McKeone and Andrew Motion more than a year ago that the Arts Council was to change its policy drastically and help individual serious writers. I'm still waiting for any evidence of this change.

1. *How much do you think a writer needs to live on?*

I think what a writer needs to live on is the same as what a postman or a doctor or a farmer needs to live on. What about the National Average Wage? Grants to writers should take account of dependents.

2. *Do you think a serious writer can earn this sum by his writing, and if so, how?*

No. Most serious writers can't earn anything like £20,000 a year. In Eire they recognise this and help with grants and also tax exemption. A few serious writers can obviously make more than this.

3. If not, what do you think is the most suitable second occupation for him?

If a writer can't make £20,000, his or her most suitable occupation will be some form of criminal activity. Personally, I'm against violent crime and the peddling of hard drugs. But when literature fails you, burglary or pot-selling may see you through. Please don't steal from your fellow-writers or any other member of the under-class. Rob the rich.

4. Do you think literature suffers from the diversion of a writer's energy into other employments or is enriched by it?

Literature is a full-time job.

5. Do you think the State or any other institution should do more for writers?

One hell of a lot more, and quick about it. All institutions which teach literature should pay wages to a writer to get on with his or her writing. They pay lots of people to teach literature, let them pay one to make it. (I include schools as well as colleges.)

6. Are you satisfied with your own solution of the problem and have you any specific advice to give to young people who wish to earn their living by writing?

I can only contribute my one-eyed solutions. I'm not satisfied with them. I want to see some bloody enthusiasm for the work of living writers and some understanding of their struggles from those who are meant to help artists. My advice to young people who wish to earn their living by writing is to learn a musical instrument and start singing.

From the *New Statesman*, 30 September 1994

Wages for Writers: The Six Hundred

'Last year I advised on a shortlist of five poets for a £15,000
bursary. Two of those poets had total earnings in 1992 of less
than £2,000; the richest had earned £15,000, almost all of it
from journalism not poetry.

'There is still a romantic idea of poets living "close to the
edge", but this often means no more than living on the breadline, consumed in petty squabbles about unpaid bills. Most
poets, unsurprisingly, can stand it only so long. After that, they
accept they're going to have to make a living in some other
fashion, and their poetry is written in the margins, from stolen
time, on the side.' Blake Morrison in *Letters*, the Journal of the
Royal Society of Literature.

But why should they accept it? Writing is a serious art. To write
poems or plays or novels you need time. You also need food and
shelter and, therefore, some kind of income. What the hell can you
do? To write well you need to experiment, to think, to read widely.
Writing well is a full-time job. So why aren't good poets, playwrights
and novelists paid regular wages?

Some of them would refuse. They're happy to write in spare hours
grabbed from the weekend. Or they're West End playwrights with
huge royalties. Or bestselling novelists. Leave them out of the
account. Most serious writers in Britain are struggling financially
most of their lives.

I have an experimental scheme to propose. It's called The Six
Hundred. It works like this. 200 poets, 200 playwrights and 200
writers of fiction are chosen by committees composed of a cross-
section of writers.

Each of these writers is paid a salary of £20,000 a year for five
years. At the end of the five years this will be renewed, unless the
writer has died, stopped writing to any marked degree, or wants to
opt out of the scheme.

Each writer will sign a contract. Half of any money earned by sale of poems, production of plays, royalties from novels – or in any other way – will go into the pool from which the writers are paid. The scheme will cost £12 million a year.

Where will the £12 million come from? My favourite method is a tax on all advertising. Advertising preys on the arts – it takes the works of Edward Lear and William Shakespeare and corrupts their words in the public mind, incessantly pounding away its greedy messages. Advertising, which often has artistic pretensions, is the opposite of art. Literature is the search for truth: advertising is the search for money. A tax on advertising would easily raise £12 million a year.

This could be boosted by the imposition of copyright on all out-of-copyright writers. Anthologists would have to pay to use poems by Keats or Milton, theatres and publishers would pay royalties for Shakespeare and Dickens – all into The Six Hundred Fund.

I know this is an awfully embarrassing subject, England. Traditionally, poets either had private incomes and wrote epics or else starved in garrets. Money is only mentioned in connection with writers when they win a huge advance or a literary prize – which is as likely as winning the pools . . . into the Valley of Wealth/Rode the Six Hundred?

Not exactly. But most writers and their families would much prefer a level income to the present roller-coaster ride or the awful trudge of the freelance today. Those who don't needn't volunteer for The Six Hundred.

In my time I've seen an incredible amount of artistic talent flattened by financial pressure – young writers in despair and old distinguished writers dying in poverty.

B. S. Johnson was one of the finest novelists Britain has produced this century. He couldn't earn enough to live on from his books. The struggle became too much. Bryan Johnson killed himself.

Some of our best poets, famous and honoured, spent their old age in poverty. Most of the help they got came from slightly luckier fellow poets. Hugh McDiarmid, Basil Bunting and George Barker – hadn't they earned a comfortable old age?

(I'm aware of all sorts of other groups both in and outside Britain who are even more in need and who can't be helped by such a small-scale scheme. I'm not forgetting them. But the plights of the unemployed here and starving refugees abroad should be tackled alongside the cause of signalmen and writers. These are not alternatives – justice is a universal need.)

The Six Hundred scheme is the first draft of a proposal. It needs to be developed by 600 imaginations and a few business brains. (When you make your contribution, please state your occupation and if you have a regular wage or salary.) The 600 will take a long time to establish. But, as the old song nearly says, we can get it if we really want.

ADRIAN MITCHELL *is a poet, playwright and children's author. His most recent books include* Blue Coffee: Poems 1985–1996, *which was a Poetry Book Society Choice and was shortlisted for the T. S. Eliot Prize for Poetry, and* Heart on the Left: Poems 1953–1984.

Blake Morrison

1. *How much do you think a writer needs to live on?*

Most writers I know would like to earn as much as barristers, have a dread of earning as little as newspaper delivery boys, and end up somewhere in between. What they say they need – anything from £10,000 to £50,000 a year – depends almost entirely on their circumstances. If you're single, without dependents, you can get by on very little; it's not so easy once there's a pram, or buggy, in the hall. Temperament comes into it, too (some writers are frugal, others sybaritic), and the choice of where you live (rents and mortgages on London property can soon eat up an advance). It doesn't help to have ex-partners or expensive habits; alimony and alcoholism don't come cheap. It does help to have an earning partner and/or supportive parents; throughout my studenty twenties – while I wrote poems, completed a doctorate, and did bits of teaching – I was subsidised by my dad, who 'lent' me money and cars.

Incidentally, I'm resistant to the idea of 'the writer' being in 'need' of anything, if this implies that writers are elite beings with unique requirements deserving of special privileges. When *Horizon* asked the question 50–odd years ago, most authors were assumed to belong to an upper-middle-class elite; their 'essential' outlay might include weekend house parties, a cellar stocked with rare clarets, and the best seats at the opera. These days assumptions are very different. A writer doesn't need any more than the next person (and often gets by on less).

2. *Do you think a serious writer can earn this sum by his writing, and if so, how?*

It depends how serious, or what kind of serious. Poets, the most dedicated of all writers, can't survive by poetry alone, even if their work sells comparatively well and they flog themselves by giving readings several times a week. Biographers have been known to command enormous advances, but even in the 1980s this was true only for a handful. Novelists sometimes do better. If their books become bestsellers, or are optioned for film; if they've a pushy agent, or a bountiful publisher; if they've sufficient chic to branch out into other kinds of writing (Hollywood screenplays, restaurant or opinion columns) and aren't destroyed by it – then they may earn substantial amounts. But only the foolhardy enter the profession expecting to live by serious literature alone, and only the lucky or exceptionally gifted succeed.

3. *If not, what do you think is the most suitable second occupation for him?*

I used to want to be a cab-driver: a chance to get out of the house, a dream of movement and open roads, and all those stories and characters you could pick up and then drop again within minutes (unlike the stories and characters in the work in progress – or not in progress – at home). But this was just a youthful Scorsese-induced fantasy, and I soon dropped it, along with fantasies of other professions I was mentally or physically not cut out for, from accountant and brain surgeon at one end to gigolo and water-ski instructor at the other. The reality has been humdrum: I've supported myself either by journalism or teaching or both. I don't think they're ideal occupations for a writer; something that stretches the body, not the mind, would surely be preferable. But they seem to be the work most writers get. I envy those with jobs that seem to enrich and feed back into their writing – like the American poet Thomas Lynch, who runs the family funeral business. But perhaps the work in itself is neither here nor there. Even lecturing has produced some excellent novels (*Lucky Jim*, *The History Man*), being a journalist, too (*Scoop*, *Miss Lonelyhearts*). The trick is to be both inside the whale and outside it at the same time, to absorb the detail but not to be absorbed by it. Which brings me to . . .

4. *Do you think literature suffers from the diversion of a writer's energy into other employments or is enriched by it?*

. . . the danger of being consumed by the day job. This is a real danger, if you take the job seriously, and try to do it well, which is what you're being paid for, after all. Employers may be fools, but they don't like to look foolish, and the days of the licensed office jester are gone: as a teacher, you're expected to teach (not just anecdotalise or dole out sherry), and as a journalist to produce reliable copy, on time. The advent of the league-table mentality in education, and the new technology in journalism, have only increased such pressures. You can't leave the work to others while you sneak off for a quick sonnet; you have to earn your keep.

Lack of time for my own writing was one of the reasons why – after 15 years of working in newspaper offices – I was glad to go freelance. For the first eight of those years, as a part-timer, I'd been able to write stuff of my own. But once I became a full-time literary editor, I wrote nothing but occasional book reviews and profiles for the next six years. Instead of carrying ideas for poems in my head, I carried ideas for editorial commissions. Where once I'd stood in the shower and seen it as a sunflower and wondered whether that would work as a metaphor or had someone else used it already, now I stood there and worried who should review the new Nadine Gordimer, the new Gore Vidal, the new Gabriel Garcia Marquez. I don't blame journalism for this; I blame having a job. I'm sure if I'd gone into university teaching, or librarianship, or carpentry, it would have been the same.

The problem of balancing 'real' work with hack work is more or less insuperable, especially now that book reviewing, the work which writers do best and most naturally, pays so badly (on most literary pages, £150–200 for 1,000 words, which would mean writing over 100,000 words annually, or the equivalent of two novels, to make a living).

To sum up: most writers either burn out from the exhaustion of having a day job or implode from the poverty, loneliness and solipsism of not having one.

5. *Do you think the State or any other institution should do more for writers?*

I think the State could do more for writers, even if this just means more of what it does already: supporting quality, independent publishing houses, giving grants and bursaries, and generally making writers feel they're not completely wasting their time. Law firms and supermarket chains have recently begun to employ poets, and good on them. But if the State values literature, it can't leave everything to private enterprise. For instance, we're desperately short of a monthly literary magazine to publish new writing, especially short stories: I'd like to see public money channelled into the creation of one.

6. *Are you satisfied with your own solution of the problem and have you any specific advice to give to young people who wish to earn their living by writing?*

I earn my living by writing, and feel very fortunate. But not all that writing is writing I'm especially eager to do and I'm never sure which commissions will turn out to be worthwhile. So I don't think I've solved the problem yet, and even if I were to solve it I'm sure any solution would be temporary.

My advice to a young writer would be: to believe (when writing) that literature is the most valuable thing in the world; to remember (when not writing) that the world values it little or not at all.

BLAKE MORRISON *is a poet and author and a former literary editor of the* Independent on Sunday. *His account of his father's death from cancer,*

And when did you last see your father?, *was the winner of the 1993 Esquire/Volvo/Waterstone's Non-Fiction Award, and was followed in 1997 by* As If, *a meditation on the Bulger case.* Too True, *a collection of essays, was published in April 1998.*

Tim Parks

1. How much do you think a writer needs to live on?

Reason not the need, is what my wife says. And I repeat it to my agent. Presumably he to my publisher. You get what you can. I imagine I can survive on as little as anyone and perhaps would like as much as most (would like!).

2. Do you think a serious writer can earn this sum by his writing, and if so, how?

'Serious' is as vague a piety as 'need'. Much of what passes for serious is fatuous. And occasionally commands high prices. Much of what is candidly fatuous sells very little. The market is completely uneven. When you write a book you are paying a high price in terms of time and effort for a lottery ticket. This makes it exciting. You might make an excellent living, or not get published at all. Or first one then the other turn and turn about. The upside is that it's never entirely your fault. The downside is there's little you can do. Which at least frees you to do what you want. Meanwhile you can mull over acceptance speeches for the Nobel, or think how to explain to the kids that you can't afford whatever it is they are inevitably clamouring for.

3. If not, what do you think is the most suitable second occupation for him?

Few begin their working lives as money-making novelists, so most already have some form of occupation by the time they publish. They must learn to balance one life against the other. Any occupation compatible with two or three hours writing a day will be suitable, with the exception of those most generally offered to writers: journalism, reviewing and creative writing courses. Journalism is as antithetical to writing as republicanism to royalty. Reviewing frequently obliges one to read the worst rather than best and even if you don't indulge in sour grapes you will certainly be accused of doing so. Exceptions are when they allow you to say a word or two in favour of someone you already admire. As for creative writing courses, if I were ordered to imagine what would best undermine the talent of a young person with a vocation for writing, I would say, the creative writing course. And if I were tempted to fantasise an unfortunate setback for someone I was foolish enough to consider a rival, I would say, let him teach a creative writing course. Living as I have in Italy for most of my adult life, I have always found translation a not unpleasant necessity, so long as the book you're working on is good. The danger is that it's so much easier to translate than to write, or at least so obvious what has to be done, that you tend to do more of it than you should.

4. *Do you think literature suffers from the diversion of a writer's energy into other employments or is enriched by it?*

Again, the business of 'literature suffering' is a horrible piety. There will always be some people mad enough to spend as long as it takes and as much as it takes to get the result they want. We don't need to worry about these things. I have always thought that the most essential energy for a writer is rancour. It's the only one that will ever give you the stubbornness you need if you're to make a long haul of it. Employment has the advantage of nourishing this most vital of impulses.

5. *Do you think the State or any other institution should do more for writers?*

No, no and no. Agents and publishers are one thing, application forms another. The only people giving you money for your work should be people who like it, or who think that enough other people will like it for them, over however long a period, to make money out of it. Any nebulous notion of giving money to writers because it is 'a good thing to do' can only lead to favouritism, nepotism and, even worse, political manipulation. The only thing that might sensibly be changed in the way authors earn at present is the publishers' aberrant use of advances. The original idea of the advance was presumably to allow the author to live while his book was prepared for publication. The system at present is mad.

Such large advances are paid to lure some authors to a publishing house that all the publicity budget inevitably goes their way in order to make sure that sales figures justify what has been paid. Perhaps a more standard notion of what an advance might be and then more reliance on royalties would make better sense. That said, I see absolutely no way the situation can change. The contemporary market demands stars. Large advances are a way of creating them. I just want part of the action.

6. *Are you satisfied with your own solution of the problem and have you any specific advice to give to young people who wish to earn their living by writing?*

If I said I was satisfied my agent might sit back, my wife might quote the remark in court when seeking to have me interned in some home or other. The children would be upset. They have friends whose fathers are dentists and accountants. That said, I am not dissatisfied. A nice flat, three excellent children, a couple of functional cars, pleasant students at the university where I put in an hour or two's teaching, a little bit of translation, long hours entirely on my own thinking what I want to think. But there is no need to give advice. Those who want to write badly enough will exhaust themselves until they make it or fail. Equally honourably. And as to these questions in general, they are merely an opportunity for chat. Nobody genuinely asking them would ever be satisfied with the answers. Anybody who has answered them for himself will know that the solution for others will be different. An artist's arrangement with money, the world and his work has to do with deep adjustments of the spirit over long periods of time and in reaction to all the peculiar circumstances that make up an individual destiny. This is what makes it so difficult and so exciting.

TIM PARKS *is the author of eight novels, including* Europa, *which was shortlisted for the 1997 Booker Prize. He has also written two works of non-fiction,* Italian Neighbours *and* An Italian Education, *and has translated novels by Alberto Moravia, Antonio Tabucchi, Italo Calvino and Roberto Calasso.*

Don Paterson

1. *How much do you think a writer needs to live on?*

Writers, however they might start out and whatever class allegiances they may retain, belong, practically by definition, to the middle classes – largely because the cultivation of one taste almost invariably leads to the refinement of all the others. Anyone, then, with middle-class tastes is going to aspire to a middle-class income. In persistently falling miles short of one they are likely to be a bit miserable, which needn't affect the quality of the work adversely, but will, starting in their late twenties, probably begin to affect their health and as a consequence their productivity; a state of perennial disappointment is not conducive to either a long life or a large oeuvre. The fact of our getting paid for this article in book tokens tacitly *assumes* this middle-class status, otherwise the gesture would be offensive in its irony, whereas it's merely ironic. Poets, in particular, learn to reconcile themselves quickly to a big gap between what they need and what they're going to get. I know well-known writers who barely clear 5k a year – almost none of this in the form of a publisher's advance – and others in their late middle age who still live in rented accommodation. (In Scotland and the north of England, incidentally, this is no kind of stigma. For various historical, cultural and economic reasons, the Chateau Lafite – okay, the Jacob's Creek – and the gallery-going tend to supplement, not supplant the beer and the football. Class defection seems to be more of a Home Counties or post-Oxbridge phenomenon.) Poets develop the knack for living on next to nothing early in their careers, so to hit a regular income of 10–15k *feels* like you've joined the middle classes. It's all terribly relative. But the main thing writers need is time to write without having to get up to answer the door to see off the wolves or Porlock debt-collectors every five minutes – and to write in a warm room with books, a decent word-processor and a telephone. 10–12k p.a. minimum for a single person, and a good bit more if there's kids involved, ought to do it, I would think.

2. *Do you think a serious writer can earn this sum by his writing, and if so, how?*

It shouldn't be impossible for good novelists to earn 15k or so p.a., thanks to the relative popularity of their medium, although I suspect I'm being incredibly naive. Poets will always find it nearly impossible, and can only do so by tearing around the country giving public readings, doing residencies, running workshops and teaching schoolchildren – which, if you're either got kids yourself or are getting on a bit, is simply not an option.

3. *If not, what do you think is the most suitable second occupation for him?*
4. *Do you think literature suffers from the diversion of a writer's energy into other employments or is enriched by it?*

If they don't have a second career, something that a) allows them to think about their work while engaged in something relatively mindless but not soul-destroying (gardening? I have no idea), or b) lets them put the skills they've developed to meaningful use – perhaps something that increases the public understanding or promulgation of good literature: education, librarianship, arts admin., editing, publishing, bookselling or writing decent genre stuff. As opposed to simultaneously depressing themselves and muddying the river with *meaningless* work, i.e. hack journalism, advertising copywriting or third-rate, embittered non-academic criticism. The idea that we should 'broaden our experience' by doing some kind of proper job has always been extraordinarily popular, especially among non-writers, for whom our relaxed hours, alcoholism and hypochondria have always been taken as a sign of moral laziness. Good artists don't have to broaden their experience. They make things up. When Delacroix wanted to paint a tiger, he used his cat as a model and made it big and stripy; it turned out pretty well.

5. *Do you think the State or any other institution should do more for writers?*

The first thing the state could do is stop closing down the libraries. The way Arts Council bursaries are handed out is a wee bit daft, as you have to propose a specific project; for poets, many of us are just writing one big book that we publish in instalments, so it's often fairly meaningless to talk about the next book as a 'project'. The A.C., in recent years, has perhaps been too attracted to insane cross-disciplinary collaborations. It's still easier to get money for that hypertext-poetry-with-throat-singing-and-freeform-macramé project than for anything sensible.

Ideally, though, it would be good to set up something along the lines of the Irish model, where good writers are voted into a kind of Royal Academy thing, and rewarded by a small annual stipend of a few thousand on condition of their continued residence – simply to acknowledge their contribution to the cultural life of the country. This should be means-tested, of course, but the whole scheme still prestigious enough for VAT-registered authors to feel honoured to be part of it anyway. A million or so a year to keep 250 of our poorest and best writers off the breadline doesn't seem much to ask. The danger is creating yet another undemocratic charmed circle, but there are ways of legislating against this. Several prizes are hopelessly ageist – the Eric Gregory Awards for poets under thirty comes to mind – and very unfair on those women (in particular, but men too) who choose to have their children in their twenties, and so might not hit their stride until forty or so.

6. *Are you satisfied with your own solution of the problem and have you any specific advice to give to young people who wish to earn their living by writing?*

I'm lucky as I can do something else when I can't write, so my solution isn't typical or useful. Generally the only answer seems to be *say yes to everything* – keep as many plates spinning as you can while somehow keeping the real writing sacrosanct. No advice to young writers except that young poets, at least, should remember to love the poetry more than they love the idea of being a successful poet; that way they can't lose. And, since poetry should be their one true faith, they shouldn't write prose unless – better, *until* – they absolutely have to.

DON PATERSON'S *first collection of poems,* Nil Nil, *was awarded the 1993 Forward Poetry Prize. The winner of the Arvon Poetry Competition for his poem 'A Private Bottling', he has also recorded three albums with his folk/ jazz ensemble, Lammas. His second collection of poems,* God's Gift to Women, *was published in May 1997 and was awarded the T. S. Eliot Prize for Poetry 1997.*

Michèle Roberts

1. *How much do you think a writer needs to live on?*

As much as anybody else. Writers are part of humanity. We don't
need special treatment. The gross inequalities in our culture favour
the rich at the poor's expense and I wish we had a government
brave enough to tackle that. I agree with George Orwell in wishing
that everybody could simply earn the same. The hidden, secret,
time-consuming work of childcare should be valued economically.
It's very hard for mothers of young children to write full-time.

2. *Do you think a serious writer can earn this sum by his writing, and if
so, how?*

A serious writer should no longer be referred to as he but as he or
she. I think it's very difficult for most writers to earn enough to live
on, since only a few get big enough advances to live on while writing
books. I didn't mind being poor for my first fifteen years or so of
writing; I saw it as part of my apprenticeship, one of the sacrifices I
was prepared to make. I didn't want to write in order to make
money; that was like a bonus. Life was very hard, but a writer doesn't
have to be particularly materialistic. Voluntary poverty, as opposed
to imposed poverty, was fine for us when we were young, back in the
sixties. The only thing that mattered to me was having enough *time*
to write; it was in that context I needed money. If you're desperate
to make money from writing you'd have to become cynical and try
to write a bestseller. Can this be planned for? It seems to me a result

rather than an aim. It's marvellous to have lots of readers, but this shouldn't be in conflict with writing the very best book you possibly can, whether that's what gets labelled as highbrow or lowbrow. Writers would earn far more if we got a higher share of royalties. Given that it's we who create the indispensable product that keeps the publishing / marketing / distribution / bookselling industries afloat, I think it's disgraceful that we get only 7% or 10% of the sale price. Writers are perceived as being greedy when they ask for big advances but at least they're getting some money to live on and not just that feeble 10%.

3. *If not, what do you think is the most suitable second occupation for him?*

I think when you need to make extra money, in order to live, you take what you can find. I can't speak for other people, since everyone's different. I took part-time work, and lived very cheaply, in order to make time to write. I couldn't afford commercial rents or a mortgage so I lived in communal houses, and in a squat at one time. Good, wild times, sometimes difficult and painful; that was the way it was. I worked part-time as a researcher, pregnancy tester and counsellor, journalist, computer clerk, teacher of evening classes and of creative writing. I had the odd Writing Fellowship, in Lambeth and in Bromley, at the University of East Anglia, at Nottingham Trent University. The latter was brilliant, because all I had to do was write my novel; I am extremely grateful. All these jobs were useful because I learned so much from them, and from the people I worked with. Now that I make a successful living from writing, I still enjoy writing book reviews, because it's lovely sitting thinking about writing, and I enjoy the radio work I do for the BBC now and again. I'm lucky enough to have the time to write most days, except when I'm working on a radio programme, but I quite value those sorties out into the world for odd jobs. It keeps you in touch with other people's reality. If I had my time all over again, I think I would have been a part-time gardener or cook. I'm certainly better at that than at filing. If you've got a talent for digging, then you should dig. When you're in the throes of writing a novel, you might want to go at it full-time, but in between books it's fun to go out and do something else for a bit. Writers shouldn't be cut off from other people. I used to laugh at the male Marxists who intoned how important it was for intellectuals to have some experience of physical labour. People who do childcare and housework have plenty of that. What's very difficult is having to combine working at your own speed and rhythm, when you're writing a book, with working at someone else's, when you're doing part-time work. It's not just a question of money, but about inner freedom. One of the big bonuses for artists (apart from meeting publishers' deadlines etc.) is being able to create your own structure and style of working; not being chained so much to the capitalist machine.

4. *Do you think literature suffers from the diversion of a writer's energy into other employments or is enriched by it?*

It's difficult thinking of ideal scenarios, so please forgive me if I keep referring to my own experience. It's probably clear from what I said above that I don't think it's necessarily a bad thing to do some other kinds of work besides writing, as long as you don't feel desperate and frustrated about losing too much time for writing. I am certainly much happier now that I don't have to work in an office filling in computer dockets. That wasn't in itself a terrible job but I just didn't want to have to do it. I enjoyed doing bits of teaching and journalism but, again, I'm glad I could stop. I got stale in the end. Whereas, with writing, you're always creating something new. But I don't think *anyone* should have to do a soul-destroying job. I don't think artists should be automatically or artificially privileged. We're in there with everybody else. But perhaps we should be more open about the sacrifices we make in order to pursue our art; other people are often very envious of us being able to be artists or writers, and jealously assume we've had it all handed to us on a plate, and don't acknowledge the struggles and costs involved. That's why this survey is a good idea.

5. *Do you think the State or any other institution should do more for writers?*

Given that the State spends vast amounts of taxpayers' money on idiotic projects like missiles, arms and the Millennium Dome, I'd be quite happy to see some of that money clawed back and given to writers instead; also to anyone else who needed it. We should invest in our writers just as we agree it's wise to invest in education and health. I wouldn't want faceless bureaucrats to be in charge of dishing out grants, however; it's much better to have constantly changing panels of the artists themselves involved. The Arts Council has been doing its best, on a restricted budget, to help the few writers it can. The Paul Hamlyn Foundation, which is not a state body, has been giving some large awards, which really help the people involved. I should like to see sponsors from business or industry, for example, not only sponsoring events but writers too; the money could be channelled via a writers' panel so that you wouldn't have to feel personally obliged to write a novel in praise of your patron! It would also be marvellous to have residencies and fellowships where you didn't have to wear yourself out teaching creative writing most of the time but could actually get on with your work. This is becoming increasingly rare. More universities could be encouraged to have writers in residence too. But you *must* be given ample time to write or you're simply being exploited.

6. *Are you satisfied with your own solution of the problem and have you any specific advice to give to young people who wish to earn their living by writing?*

I think you have to validate the choices you've made in the past or else you waste too much time in regrets. So, yes, I think I solved the problem adequately; I felt I had no other choice than to manage the way I did. My advice to you would-be writers is: get yourself a good agent; don't be too grateful to your publisher even if you have a lovely editor; if you want to be rich go into the City instead; be prepared to take odd jobs; remember you can have a marvellous time without pots of money. I'm sure much of what I've said sounds pompous and priggish, so I hope readers will forgive me.

MICHÈLE ROBERTS *is the author of seven novels, including* Flesh & Blood *and* Daughters of the House, *which was shortlisted for the 1992 Booker Prize and won the W. H. Smith Literary Award. She has also published a collection of short stories,* During Mother's Absence, *three books of poetry and has co-authored four volumes of short stories.*

Jane Rogers

1. *How much do you think a writer needs to live on?*

There's no reason why a writer should be given special financial rewards, but it seems equally unreasonable that he or she should be financially penalised for choosing to write. Writers are as necessary as bakers or architects. Depending on where they live, a writer with a family needs about £20,000 a year.

2. *Do you think a serious writer can earn this sum by his writing, and if so, how?*

The word 'serious' here has unfortunate connotations. (Financially unsuccessful? Difficult? As opposed to bestselling and popular?) I imagine most writers, including comic ones, are serious about what they write; obviously the popular and successful ones – even the successful literary ones – earn plenty. But the majority of us have to cobble together a living. Yes, it can all be done by writing, but it might be that only a small part of that income will come from writing what the writer really wants to write. Writing novels is an addiction, a habit, which I have to help to support by teaching and writing other things which pay better and (theoretically) take less time.

3. *If not, what do you think is the most suitable second occupation for him?*

God knows what's a suitable occupation for a writer, other than writing. Something physical – delivering the post, cleaning windows, gardening? The other difficulty with being a writer, apart from income, is the solitude; it makes sense for the second occupation to involve human contact. Teaching is sometimes OK. Teaching writing seems a good option, though it's frustrating at times because it can muddle your wits for your own work.

4. *Do you think literature suffers from the diversion of a writer's energy into other employments or is enriched by it?*

There's no straight answer to this; work that isn't writing has proved inspirational for some and pointless for others. Most writers need contact with the world, to have something to *write* about – paid employment seems a reasonable way of maintaining that contact, but it does erode writing time.

5. *Do you think the State or any other institution should do more for writers?*

The Arts Council Bursaries for novelists are a good thing, but they are only necessary because most novelists at some point in their career are prevented from writing by the lack of money. Why *should* the state pay writers? We're not sick or unemployed, we are actually producing something the public wants. Paying us according to the size of audience we deliver isn't necessarily appropriate, in that there are minority tastes in literature as in everything else. Even if it's only going to sell a few thousand copies, or be broadcast at 2am, a piece of writing may be the first work of a writer who will become very important; it may contain elements which will inspire or affect other artists; and it will anyway feed the imaginations of the minority who do read or hear it.

Maybe we should think about who really profits (financially) from writers. Writers produce the raw material which is flogged by publishers, booksellers, radio, film and TV companies. The jobs of all the people employed in these trades depend on us. And all of these businesses – despite their protestations – make profits. Not one of them is a charity. They make better profits than writers do and they pay themselves better wages; compare the salary of a commissioning editor in a publishing house with the income of one of his writers, over ten years, or the salary of a TV executive (or even a lowly script editor) with the writer of the script. There must be a way of recapturing some of the profit generated by the person who lays the golden egg, and channelling it back to other writers – both new and established – who need it. Ideally, it should come in the form of commissions to write specific pieces those writers *want* to write, be it prose or drama. The resulting work would be the writer's to sell wherever he/she chose. The system could be similar to the Arts Council bursaries, but administered by the Society of Authors and Writers' Guild (or even the Royal Society of Literature, which seems to lack a proper function) – but it would be financed by those companies who profit from writers and need to keep them alive. Some profits from books which are out of copyright could also be siphoned into this fund, as D. S. Savage suggested back in 1946. And it shouldn't be seen as a handout, but as payment for writing.

6. *Are you satisfied with your own solution of the problem and have you any specific advice to give to young people who wish to earn their living by writing?*

Sometimes yes, frequently no. Looking back, it seems to me that writing novels and looking after young children combined very well for me – I wrote fast and furiously when my partner was looking after them or when they were asleep, and I taught evening classes and part-time to supplement the novel advances. Children are a brilliant escape from being alone with a bit of paper; and writing is the perfect antidote to children. And in comparison to both, the teaching was a doddle. Recently, I've made more of my writing income by writing for TV and that's not a solution I'd recommend to anyone. Yes, you do get paid; you get enthusiastic, you write – then you attend endless meetings where all sorts of helpful suggestions are made to turn your script into something you never dreamt of, which no-one is going to make anyway. I've been told the BBC make one in eight of the scripts they commission (that's written, finished products). Leading you to believe you would have been better employed breaking rocks.

Advice for aspiring writers? None. If they're compelled to write, they'll find a way to do it. If not, it's a tedious and lonely way to make an erratic living, and they'll soon discover that and get a job that pays proper wages.

JANE ROGERS *is the author of five novels, including* Her Living Image, Promised Lands, *and* Mr Wroe's Virgins, *which she also adapted for television. Her television play,* Dawn and the Candidate, *won a Samuel Beckett Award. She was made a Fellow of the Royal Society of Literature in 1994, and currently teaches the Novel in the Creative Writing MA at Sheffield Hallam University.*

Bernice Rubens

1. *How much do you think a writer needs to live on?*

A writer is no different from any other earner. What he needs to live on largely depends on the volume of his responsibilities. Ideally a writer should live alone. Basically, he or she is not fit to live with. Therefore he would have only himself to keep. But this is rarely the case. The experience of marriage and parenthood is good fuel to any writer. Though we should note that few have written better about marriage and children than Jane Austen.

2. *Do you think a serious writer can earn this sum by his writing, and if so, how?*

I think that poets, unless they are universally acclaimed, would find it more difficult than a novelist. For there exists more possible spin-offs for fiction; T.V. and film adaptations, foreign translations. But for these you have to be lucky. A poet would have to depend on the sundry grants available. But, on the whole, I would think it difficult to earn a living wage from writing alone.

3. *If not, what do you think is the most suitable second occupation for him?*

A writer can take any secondary job as long as it does not depend on language. That would rule out advertising and run-of-the-mill journalism, in which pursuits little respect for language is required. A serious writer is writing all the time, whether at or outside his desk. So it doesn't really matter what secondary occupation he follows. I believe that writers must be physically fit. Personally I find writing *physically* tiring, strange as it may seem. So I need to keep in trim. I'm not thinking, God forbid, about jogging or aerobics, but we should somehow keep ourselves on the move. So avoid sedentary work. Save that for your desk. Manual work is a good idea, as long as it doesn't exhaust your energy. Work is possible with other creative artists, a carpenter perhaps, or an architect. Or simply take a mindless job on a conveyor belt. Whatever you choose to do, you stand to gain from the knowledge and society of people different from yourself. And that is bound to be enriching. Moreover, it will temporarily take the edge off your ego, and that can only be beneficial.

4. *Do you think literature suffers from the diversion of a writer's energy into other employments or is enriched by it?*

I don't honestly think a writer concerns himself with wondering whether literature is suffering because he's doing a secondary job. He has better things to think about. This is the sort of question that reviewers and biographers go to town on. No matter. Everyone has to earn a living. As far as I can see, the only drawback to secondary employment is loss of time. And as a corollary of that, a loss of continuity. A writer needs both.

5. *Do you think the State or any other institution should do more for writers?*

This is the big one. And my answer is an unequivocal 'No'. I don't think writers are special, and therefore they are not entitled to special pleading. Nobody forces you to be a writer. It is your own decision, your own compulsion, and you must be prepared to reap the joys and disappointments of that pursuit, I don't think that the majority of readers think that writers are special. What worries me are the writers who think they are. And I don't think this attitude can be awfully good for their fiction. A writer should take his work very seriously, but a writer who takes *himself* seriously is a pain in the arse. I am one of the Vice-Presidents of P.E.N., and I am involved in the situation of writers in prison all over the world. Known and unknown, writers are incarcerated for their compulsion to express themselves freely. In many countries they are tortured, and in some put to death. All of them have had their pens taken away. In England we still have the blessed freedom to write and to publish. No writer enjoying such freedom can pick up his pen without at least an *awareness* of those countless words and images that have been muzzled by censorship and torture. I think that if we are haunted by this awareness, as we should be, the whole notion of state subsidy is faintly obscene.

6. *Are you satisfied with your own solution of the problem and have you any specific advice to give to young people who wish to earn their living by writing?*

I have never regarded being a writer as a problem. I do it because there is nothing else I can do. Therefore the notion of a *solution* is not viable. I've been lucky in my career, and I stress the luck of it. I've written twenty-one novels, and from the fourth onwards, I was able to earn my living by writing. But whether I would be earning or not, I'd still, somehow or other, be writing. I do a reasonable amount of teaching, because writing gives me so much pleasure and I like to turn others on to that activity. And there is always the hope that you will discover an exciting talent. I advise the younger students to go to university if possible, but if they want to be writers, on no account should they read English. I suggest Biology. I myself read English and I did not start writing till I was over thirty. I was so much in awe of our great 19th-century novel tradition, I found it difficult to write with Jane Austen at my elbow and the Brontës breathing down my neck. I think that the fact that American writers are not so bogged down by tradition is the reason why they produce so much more exciting fiction that we do in England. They can afford a greater audacity, a greater nerve, a greater daring.

If a young person were to ask me if he could earn a living by writing, I would deduce that the writing itself was of secondary importance. I would advise him to study accountancy – a far more reliable career.

BERNICE RUBENS' *novels include* The Elected Member, *for which she won the 1970 Booker Prize, and* A Five Year Sentence. *Two of her novels,* I Sent a Letter to My Love *and* Madame Sousatzka, *have been turned into films, and one,* Mr Wakefield's Crusade, *into a television series. Her most recent novel,* The Waiting Game, *was published in August 1997.*

Will Self

I feel this entire exercise is essentially invidious and possibly even specious. The whole nature of artistic endeavour is to promote the existence of elites; without elites there would be no excellence, no talent. So, while one might well be a social egalitarian, one is never a cultural egalitarian. Any exercise which is intended to palliate the harsh fact that talentless people are without talent represents as much a waste of human endeavour as an advertising agency in full flood!

1. *How much do you think a writer needs to live on?*

As much as anybody else. J. G. Ballard always said that before writing *Empire of the Sun* he earned about as much as an English G.P.; and after Spielberg made the movie he earned about as much as an American G.P. I think these represent the acceptable poles of remuneration for writers.

2. *Do you think a serious writer can earn this sum by his writing, and if so, how?*

'Serious' is a ludicrous ascription; some of the most facetious writers I know are also the most profoundly serious. I certainly don't think it's possible to earn a G.P.'s salary writing books that are intended to serve posterity rather than the present, but I also happen to think that writers who set out to achieve this end often produce a load of bollocks. Indeed, when I hear a writer utter the word 'posterity' I reach for my gun.

3. *If not, what do you think is the most suitable second occupation for him?*

Any occupation will do. For the contemplative sort perhaps night-watchman or Buddhist monk; for the active and socially inquisitive, parent, journalist, home help, or social worker will do. To be allowed to write and to have an audience is always a privilege – never a right.

4. *Do you think literature suffers from the diversion of a writer's energy into other employments or is enriched by it?*

Both can be the case. Certainly, if a creative worker is drained by her occupations elsewhere she cannot be expected to write well, but on the whole I think writers should live as much as possible in the ordinary and commonplace world, and be subjected to the same impoverishment and enrichment as everyone else.

5. *Do you think the State or any other institution should do more for writers?*

I personally have never received any grant from the State or any other institution, so this tends to make me resistant to the idea. However, I can envisage circumstances in which writers should be offered assistance, although these would occur at the end of their careers – not the beginning.

6. *Are you satisfied with your own solution of the problem and have you any specific advice to give to young people who wish to earn their living by writing?*

There is no 'problem' to be addressed here, because there is no way of ensuring that the quality of a society's culture corresponds to anything other than the talents of the artists currently working within it. *Fin de siècle* Vienna was pretty hot in the literary stakes, but a stink hole when it came to social policy. You cannot legislate for excellence. Personally, if I were a young writer setting out I would ask myself two fundamental questions: a) Am I talented? b) Does being a professional writer matter more to me than anything else in life?

If my answers were both in the affirmative I would soldier on – but never with an expectation either of acclaim or emolument. If either answer were in the negative I would apply for a Bergson Grant. Henri Bergson – you will recall – offered the eminently sensible solution to this apparent 'problem': young writers should be offered bursaries on the strict understanding that they undertook not to write anything at all!

WILL SELF'S *first book, the short story collection* The Quantity Theory of Insanity, *won the Geoffrey Faber Memorial Prize. Subsequent books have included two novels,* My Idea of Fun *and* Great Apes, *three novellas,* Cock and Bull *and* The Sweet Smell of Psychosis, *and a collection of journalism,* Junk Mail. *His latest collection of short stories,* Tough Tough Toys for Tough Tough Boys, *was published in April 1998.*

Nicholas Shakespeare

1. *How much do you think a writer needs to live on?*

How much were writers paid in 1946 to answer these questions? £2 maximum, according to Michael Shelden, who wrote the history of *Horizon*. Today, we stand to receive £200–worth of Waterstone's vouchers. Now you cannot eat a book token, cross the sea with it, but this hundredfold increase in one's 'honorarium' provides a crude yardstick by which to compare cost-of-living figures. George Orwell reckoned a married man could live on a minimum income of £10 a week net, which becomes £520 a year – which translates to £52,000. His was the average sum (making it easy to understand why Elizabeth Bowen raised eyebrows with her stated requirement: £350,000 net does sound needy).

Speaking for myself, SWMNS, 40, living in London with a mortgage and no private income, I need a minimum of £25,000 (gross). To have a bit of a life: £35,000.

2. *Do you think a serious writer can earn this sum by his writing, and if so, how?*

I understand 'serious writer' to mean someone who writes what they want, for its own sake (fiction in my case, set usually in South America). Unless you are very lucky, you will find it difficult to earn this from advances and sales.

On the other hand, a journalist, who writes what others want, can earn good money. I was receiving upwards of £40,000 (as literary editor of the *Daily/Sunday Telegraph*) when I decided to pack it in to finish a novel. But I was careful before jumping to save as much as I could. Just as well: the novel took three years to complete and earned, eventually, a total of £17,000.

Prizes and translation rights help. But publishers are fickle and success guarantees nothing except, in Graham Greene's words, 'failure postponed'. My first novel won two prizes, was translated into ten languages. Yet only two foreign publishers bothered with the second and the rest fled as ewes from the jackal. At the moment I'm back in favour with twelve, but it would be a lunatic who counted on their loyalty. They're important to build confidence, to make you feel that you deserve to be doing this. And they don't pay enormously well. I recently sold Turkish rights for £137.50.

Films pay more, of course, but you have to work with actors.

3. *If not, what do you think is the most suitable second occupation for him?*

Anything that wakens you to the world. A job where you're going to be falling asleep is bad. It's a romantic notion that you need to wash dishes in Paris hotels. That kind of existence grinds you down. I've plucked turkeys in the Harrods' basement, sold ties at Swan & Edgar, taught English, but I cannot proclaim the experience enriched me. The goal is to find the milieu in which you feel most curious, and then do whatever you have to do in order to put yourself in a position which frees you to write.

It's tricky to be prescriptive about this. If you are someone able to compartmentalise your life, then you're fortunate. It was traditional in Connolly's day to moonlight as a schoolmaster, academic, clergyman, diplomat, anything with the prospect of a huge holiday. But these professions consume more time today.

If your ambition is to write novels, journalism is a good training ground for certain muscles. (I include film and television, which force you to think visually and in narrative terms). But you cannot master all genres. There comes a moment when you have to find the courage to go out into the arena you aspire to. If you stay too long in training you become what you do: either you find you're putting your best energy into small performances, or, a worse danger, you start treating what you do as hackwork, which is a disservice to journalism.

4. *Do you think literature suffers from the diversion of a writer's energy into other employments or is enriched by it?*

In the end, fiction is too serious to engage in part-time. It's hard to improve on Margaret Atwood's riposte to the brain-surgeon who asked what she intended to do when she retired. 'When I retire, I'm going to take up brain surgery.'

In the end, fiction is not frivolous: it's a craft. You have to approach it as a brain surgeon approaches their training. It's just that there are many more corridors leading to the surgery room and you have to find your own way through the maze. It's never going to be spelled out for you.

5. *Do you think the State or any other institution should do more for writers?*

I don't believe the State should do anything for writers unless they are a) sick, or b) well and truly washed up. It's not the State's job. I cannot think of any brilliant books which have come about from the State. The funding never goes to the right people, only to those who write brilliant applications. If you're State-sponsored, you don't learn how to get your claws in properly. You write books that nobody reads and it doesn't matter. If you're on your own, there's no safety net and you're forced to fly or fall.

On the other hand, any private assistance – a place to write in or a privately endowed fellowship – is to be welcomed. But nothing which makes you accountable on any level.

6. *Are you satisfied with your own solution of the problem and have you any specific advice to give to young people who wish to earn their living by writing?*

Am I satisfied financially? Not enormously, not when I consider the salary I gave up. Who is? But I'm finally doing what I want.

Resist as long as possible. As a child, the only model I had as a writer was my grandfather. He wrote 250 books and died penniless and heartbroken at 89 after his wife of half a century ran away. I didn't want to be like him.

Money is important, but it's important not to write for it. Follow the example of Norman Lewis who made his money first in a chain of camera shops in order to be free to write. It's wise, also a little painful maybe, to remember something else. All really good books bubble out of a person: they can't not write them, and they're not commissioned.

The former literary editor of the Daily *and* Sunday Telegraph, *Nicholas Shakespeare is the author of three novels,* The Vision of Elena Silves, The High Flyer *and* The Dancer Upstairs. *He was chosen as one of* Granta *magazine's Best of Young British Novelists in 1993 and is currently writing the authorised biography of Bruce Chatwin.*

Joan Smith

1. *How much do you think a writer needs to live on?*

The cost of being a writer has gone up enormously. Few writers still scribble on scraps of paper or bang out novels on elderly typewriters; if they do, they are unlikely to be taken seriously by publishers or editors, who expect novelists and critics to be *au fait* with computers, printers, fax machines and modems. I don't think, though, that many of them bear this in mind when negotiating payment for articles or books. Nor do they care very much how writers live, a question which always seems to strike them as vulgar on the rare occasions it is raised at all. At a time when publishing has become much more commercial, this strikes me as odd: why is it OK to think about print runs and projected sales, to cost a book down to the last item, and yet appear indifferent – hostile even – when authors point out that they have to pay the gas bill like anyone else? I'm convinced there's an element of class here, an attitude which holds that, if you're a *real* writer, you'll somehow manage to rise above the petty anxieties of everyday life and produce your books anyway.

This is, for the most part, complete rubbish. It's obvious that authors, depending on their individual circumstances, need as much as anyone else to live on. The great difference between now and the 1940s is that so few of us have the option of inherited wealth or unearned income to fall back on. I don't mind this in the least, as long as it's recognised that I also don't want to starve in a garret. I'm certainly not the kind of writer who wants to be sheltered from the world; on the contrary, my engagement in it is vital to the kind of books and articles I write. So the answer to the question of how much I personally need to live is: sufficient to cover living in London, with a garden for my cats, and have the kind of social and political life I thrive on. In other words, I should think, about the same as the editors and publishers who commission my work.

2. *Do you think a serious writer can earn this sum by his writing, and if so, how?*

I know it's possible to be a serious writer and live more or less exclusively on the income from it: possible but difficult. The trick is to be good at several different types of writing, and to avoid becoming dependent on any single source, whether it's a publisher or a newspaper. Retaining a high degree of independence – by which I mean the confidence to turn down unsuitable commissions – is essential. This is not an easy road to travel and, for most writers, takes years to achieve. Quite what one does along the way – struggle, borrow, fight off depression – is something I don't like to think about.

3. *If not, what do you think is the most suitable second occupation for him?*

Some writers manage to take on, perhaps even enjoy, other jobs. I've known poets who teach film studies and biographers who teach at universities, but no career other than writing has ever been a possibility for me. I knew I was a writer when I was eight or nine, back in junior school. So certain was I, in fact, that for years I couldn't quite understand why other people didn't immediately recognise me as a novelist, journalist, essayist. It was so obviously the cornerstone of my identity that the fact I hadn't yet written a book – my first was published when I was 32 – made very little difference to me. It's not just that I love being a writer, it's who I am. I'm sure other writers feel very differently but, if I had to do something else, my life would be unbearable – and so would I.

4. *Do you think literature suffers from the diversion of a writer's energy into other employments or is enriched by it?*

Of course literature, and writers, suffer from the diversion of energy into other employments – unless they're deliberately chosen. Not everyone wants to be a full-time writer, and that's fine. If you do, having to waste energy on other projects is intolerable. Writing is, for me at least, a balancing act between having the confidence to embark on a project, whether it's a novel or a book of essays or a regular newspaper column, and the self-doubt which makes you write and re-write until you're almost – never completely – satisfied. My ambition, whatever I'm writing, is always to narrow the gap between ambition and execution. This is difficult enough, without having to do another job and squeeze writing around it. I am in a continuous process of thinking, writing, revising, and allowing the unconscious to move ahead – especially if I'm writing a novel. I don't have the time, energy or the inclination for anything else.

The other great drain on a writer's energy is worrying about money. It isn't the writing itself which is damaged by waiting for cheques, but the ability to move smoothly between the real world and the one inside your head. Part of a writer's job is to discover from experience what eases that transition and what blocks it. The conclusion I've reached is that writers need to be organised, indeed ruthless, about making sure they are paid on time. It's hard to produce your best work when you're distracted by anxiety about your mortgage or your phone bill.

5. *Do you think the State or any other institution should do more for writers?*

No. What I do believe very passionately is that writers shouldn't be subjected to the kind of narrow cost-benefit analysis which takes no account of how they're going to live while they write a book. Editors get paid a living wage, even when they commission books whose sales are disappointing. Why should writers, uniquely, be expected to write at the very top of their ability for sums of money which even the most frugal adult cannot live on? The unspoken assumptions are that art isn't work, that writers are gentlemen and it wouldn't be quite nice to pay them a proper rate for the job – unless, perversely, they're rich and don't need it. These days, when most writers do try to survive on what they earn, small advances are a form of exploitation.

6. *Are you satisfied with your own solution of the problem and have you any specific advice to give to young people who wish to earn their living by writing?*

My solution, outlined above, works most of the time. What I'd say to young writers is that they should have confidence in themselves, and a belief in their right to be paid for what they do. Writing is more than a job, it's an enormous pleasure, but that isn't a reason for not paying authors properly.

JOAN SMITH'S *books include* Misogynies, Different for Girls: How Culture Creates Women *and* Hungry for You: From Cannibalism to Seduction – A Book of Food. *She is also the author of five Loretta Lawson novels, two of which –* A Masculine Ending *and* Don't Leave Me This Way – *have been filmed for BBC TV starring Imelda Staunton.*

Stella Tillyard

1. *How much do you think a writer needs to live on?*

Writers need as much as everybody else to live on, and like everybody else, most writers will tell you it is not enough.

2. *Do you think a serious writer can earn this sum by his writing, and if so, how?*

My earnings are at about the level of a (grossly underpaid) senior lecturer in a British university. They are made up of advances (both UK and foreign), royalties, sales of film rights, fees from journalism and the odd fillip of prize money. From the gross I take my agent's commissions, contributions to my personal pension and expenses, as well as taxes. I have a working partner, two children, no unearned income and a mortgage. Of course I don't think it is enough and of course I cast round constantly for ways of earning more. I take every job I am offered unless it is detrimental to my professional identity, and like many other writers I will always do jobs – radio work, journalism or assignments like this – which have more than a financial justification.

My major problems, that I share with many writers, are that I have no security and that I have to write against the clock to maintain a reasonable income. Frequent small advances result in frequent, small books. I believe publishers should have greater confidence, invest in talent and be prepared to wait longer for better books.

3. If not, what do you think is the most suitable second occupation for him?

Many years ago I used to be approached by modelling agencies and cannot now imagine why I was so high minded as to spurn offers to suffer for my art and build a nest-egg for my future, especially as the job demands no brain work and no heavy lifting. I did have the sense to take, equally many years ago, a highly suitable job in the Oriental Department of the Bodleian Library. My initial brief was to type out catalogue cards for the Chinese books that would arrive daily in chemically fragrant parcels from the fumigation chamber. Being dyslexic, I could barely read, much less type the translitera-tion of the titles, which seemed to consist entirely of cs and hs separated by an assortment of vowels and a flurry of hyphens.

Transferred to the frowzy Reading Room, I read books under the table while keeping up a pretence of supervising the somnolent scholars and receiving visits from friends. Quickly banned from reading and receiving, I still had one consolation: visiting the subterranean world of the Bodleian stack. The Oriental books were shelved directly under their readers' feet. But the eager Sinophiles and Sanskrit scholars could unaccountably wait an hour or more as I toured the purgatorial regions, going from level to level, where I had books concealed behind broken chairs, on top of defunct radiators and even among the originals of the carved heads that run round the Sheldonian Theatre. I was nearly sacked for taking a particularly thrilling volume about the Mongol armies home for the night, but nonetheless this was a five-star job once I had worked out the responsibilities involved. It is true that when I left, the shattered head of the division was heard to mutter that he would never hire anyone like me again, but aspiring writers might still find it worth trying.

4. Do you think literature suffers from the diversion of a writer's energy into other employments or is enriched by it?

Writers are all different. Paid work may be a diversion to some. But for others it is a psychological corrective to hours of solitude or a source of material. Still, writers of books – as opposed to journalists or poets, who occupy different branches of literature – require stretches of uninterrupted time and most give up their day jobs as soon as they can.

As for the delightful pram in the hall, which must be mentioned because it is an employment, although unpaid, Cyril Connolly was right. Not because it stunts creativity – if anything, I think the reverse – but because it takes hours and hours and acres of emotional space. Months of suburban monotony without anxiety or excitement are what most writers need for a sustained career and it is absurd to pretend that children don't disturb that.

5. *Do you think the State or any other institution should do more for writers?*

Government, business and writers' organisations should do much, much more for writing as an industry and an export. We live in one of the most literary cultures in the world, yet fail to celebrate and exploit it. Every British child spends years doing creative writing assignments of the sort that children in the US and on the Continent never see. As a result, literally millions of adults write in their spare time.

Other branches of the media business, notably film, design and fine art, have happily accepted their identification with 'New Britain', and writers should be doing the same. Britlit could be every bit as fashionable as Britart and the whole culture as well as the practitioners would benefit. Writers' organisations should be actively promoting their members to government and industry; by lobbying, for instance, for tax breaks for companies that have writers in residence. The Millennium Dome? We should be in it, and planning our contribution now: Shakespeare is probably our nation's most influential export. Booker, Whitbread and other companies that sponsor prizes could do much more to promote them, especially by creating Websites and bulletin boards for ordinary readers to join it. Poetry, which has a particularly large number of amateur practitioners, should have its own national prize. A good deal of effort is expended trying to make these prizes controversial; very little to make them fun or fashionable.

At government level, the British Council should dust itself off and set to work with agents and foreign publishers to promote those writers who sell abroad. Make it worthwhile for authors to travel – it is a job, not a holiday – and insist that their events are not simply publicity for their own works. Demand the highest intellectual quality, seek out the best performers and use them to promote unknown talent.

As for the Arts Council, I have never applied for Arts Council funding and have no idea if I am eligible. But I believe the Arts Council should fund writing with two- or three-year bursaries in a similar fashion and at comparable rates of pay to the fellowships awarded to academics by the British Academy. These bursaries are not given for poverty; they are given for specific projects and as rewards and incentives for effort and excellence. £5,000 would be completely useless to a writer such as myself. Two years funded at a reasonable level, on the other hand, could make a book significantly better as literature, and that is what writers are striving for.

6. *Are you satisfied with your own solution of the problem and have you any specific advice to give to young people who wish to earn their living by writing?*

I have no immediate solution to the problem of job security. But I have never regretted becoming a full-time writer, although I am never satisfied with my own work; for me it is a vocation as well as a job. After a spell at art college in the mid nineteen-eighties, I went in desperation to a careers service in the West End, where I filled in a long questionnaire ('Would you rather wire a 747 or arrange flowers at home?') and sat a series of aptitude tests. Ushered up in the afternoon to see a severe advisor, I was pronounced 'unemployable', and tottered out into Gloucester Place feeling desperate and useless. How can I not feel tremendously fortunate to have stumbled upon the solution of self-employment? I even fondly imagine that it has made me employable at last.

Finally, I am a great receiver of advice; it's one of my pastimes. But I think that giving it is pointless.

STELLA TILLYARD *is the author of two works of history* — Aristocrats, *a study of eighteenth-century family life, and its follow-up,* Citizen Lord, *a biography of Edward Fitzgerald. A winner of the Pevsner Prize, she has taught at Harvard (where she was a Knox Fellow) and at the UCLA.*

Claire Tomalin

1. *How much do you think a writer needs to live on?*

Writers don't take up their work to become rich, and most are poor. It is the honourable condition of the artist. I can think of about twenty-five writers I know whom I suppose earn high incomes (in writers' terms, not businessmen's terms, or publishers' or BBC executives', of course) through books or plays. But from nearly twenty-five years' service on the committee of the Royal Literary Fund I know of scores of respected writers who are desperately poor, and face penurious old age dependent on social security. The situation has grown worse over the years, there's no doubt, as reading habits and publishers have changed, losing interest in their 'middle list' writers.

V. S. Pritchett's advice in 1946 remains good: 'Be born with a small private income; or get yourself supported by a husband or wife.' Lacking either, if you choose to have no children, live without heating (and some do) and are mostly fed by friends, you might manage on £5,000 a year, although I'm not suggesting you should. Even this much is difficult for an apprentice novelist to earn, or a young poet, or a writer of non-fiction who needs to research a subject for several years. A more reasonable estimate of what you can live on if you have no responsibilities to anyone but yourself is, I'd guess, around £10,000 a year.

2. *Do you think a serious writer can earn this sum by his writing, and if so, how?*

If you are productive and publish two or three books that are well reviewed, and have an agent and a publisher who believe in you – so many ifs – this much should be possible. With any luck, more. There will be perks which are also distractions: requests to lecture, to write newspaper articles, to appear on television. Of course, you have only to fall out of favour with the public to find yourself penniless again; and it is extremely difficult to find a job when you are fifty.

3. *If not, what do you think is the most suitable second occupation for him?*

Women tend to have another occupation anyway, but it is one that fits in rather well with writing, especially if a supporting husband is involved. Lots of us began writing with children about, breaking off to cook, shop, do the washing, pick up from school. Remember Candia McWilliam's wise words, though: for each baby you lose two books you might have written. I don't know how people write books when they are working full-time at something else. I found it impossible. In 1986 I left a job as literary editor for which I was being paid £30,000 and took up full-time writing. My earnings from royalties and advances on books were very small for the first few years, but over the past six they average at about £15,000 a year. I do not regret leaving the job. On the other hand, many writers do manage to take on regular and demanding reviewing, teach in schools or have academic jobs; you have to work out your own balance and possibilities.

4. *Do you think literature suffers from the diversion of a writer's energy into other employments or is enriched by it?*

This is an old-fashioned question. In one sense, the more a writer knows the better, and employments other than writing will enrich his or her experience. Or they may stand in the way of writing. The simple process of growing older probably enriches your mind as much as anything else.

5. *Do you think the State or any other institution should do more for writers?*

What can the State do, especially now the Welfare State is being dismantled? Now is the time perhaps for Civil List pensions, which are far too small to be meaningful except as an 'honour', to be raised to proper, substantial amounts. There is a crying need for some system of pensions for writers. The Royal Literary Fund is doing something here, and looking into the possibility of doing more. In Germany the Public Lending Right system retains part of its takings for writers' pensions, a system we might imitate, at the same time beefing up our Public Lending Right payments. We should at the same time ask well-to-do writers to elect not to take their Public Lending Right payments, so that they can be ploughed back for the others.

6. *Are you satisfied with your own solution of the problem and have you any specific advice to give to young people who wish to earn their living by writing?*

I have been lucky in having moderate success with my books, although I did not start writing until I was forty. Now I wish I had more time ahead. So, my advice would be to start early, and write as much as you can while you are young and energetic. Find an agent, if possible, who understands your financial situation and is prepared to work out strategies to help you stay afloat. The odd film script may not corrupt you, but don't take on work you despise. Your true voice is what you are hoping to put out into the world, and you are seeking readers who find it so interesting that they will buy your books in order to listen to whatever story you are choosing to tell them. When they do listen, it is better than being rich.

The former literary editor of the New Statesman *and* Sunday Times, *Claire*

Tomalin is the author of six biographies, including The Life and Death of Mary Wollstonecraft *(winner of the Whitbread First Book Prize in 1974),* The Invisible Woman, Mrs Jordan's Profession, *and* Jane Austen: A Life, *which was published in September 1997.*

Rose Tremain

1. *How much do you think a writer needs to live on?*

Worrying about money interrupts, or even erodes, a writer's necessary 'dreaming time', that almost undefinable state in which the mind silently discovers, rejects, sifts and rearranges ideas and images. Thus, each individual writer needs to earn at the level at which he or she can put the subject of money into some safe, untroubled, seldom-visited compartment of the brain. Obviously, the actual amount to be earned will vary, according to temperament, age, number of dependents, size and location of house, alcohol consumption and so forth, but I would say that any writer who earns less than £10,000 a year will feel that he is poor.

2. *Do you think a serious writer can earn this sum by his writing, and if so, how?*

The whole climate in which a writer earns has changed since I began to write novels in the 1970s. Large sums of money are paid to writers now, even or especially to unknown first-time writers, whereas the sum paid to me for my first novel was £350 (less than £3000 in today's terms and the book had taken eighteen months to write). Thus, today it shouldn't be too hard for a reasonably prolific serious writer to earn at a viable level. Yet in practice, it probably is hard because a publisher's loyalty to a writer may only last through one or two 'unsuccessful' books and, if this happens, that writer will be sent back out into an Antarctica of penury and disappointment, perhaps with his stock of ideas depleted, and have to beg another publisher to take him on at a reduced fee. The only writers who will survive are the ones who can keep the loyalty of their publishers by coming up with consistently interesting, saleable work. For these people, it certainly isn't hard to earn a very reasonable income.

3. *If not, what do you think is the most suitable second occupation for him?*

Every novelist should, at the outset of his or her career at least, have a 'second arm', in the form of some other kind of writing or some other paid work. The nature of this work depends upon what the individual can bear to do. I have found, for instance, that I do not thrive, really, as a teacher, but I have always been happy to work in radio – writing features and plays. Others survive very well in university environments or as regular reviewers or TV soap writers. The Day Job is not a dishonourable idea.

4. *Do you think literature suffers from the diversion of a writer's energy into other employments or is enriched by it?*

Literature needs ideas. Whatever can furnish a writer with original ideas should be the thing that is sought. This might be 'other employment' (a teaching job in Nashville, Tennessee set my mind yodelling with crazed new thoughts) or it might not. Most writers need sufficient blank time – which is not the same thing as time employed doing something else – in which to let ideas take shape. Drive a writer into too many hours of alternative work and he will probably cease to write at all because he will be too tired. Writing novels has been compared by Joyce Carol Oates to boxing and this comparison isn't as peculiar as it looks. Novelists have to keep alert, work out a strategy, seize the unexpected, bounce from punch to punch and stay the course, even when the brain is tiring and the gumshield of self-belief has been knocked out onto the canvas. But if a novelist is writing his novels only to pay his bills, the books are

likely to be formulaic or to become so over time because his heart
and his intellect won't really be in them.

5. *Do you think the State or any other institution should do more for writers?*

The State should do more for the Arts in general. Give us more
theatre subsidy and film development and funding subsidy and new
dramatists and scriptwriters will be given the chances they need to
become the great writers of the future. But the novelist roams alone.
I'm not sure how the State can help him, except by the provision of
travel bursaries (such as the Arts Council gives) so that he can take
his roaming further and wider.

6. *Are you satisfied with your own solution of the problem and have you any
specific advice to give to young people who wish to earn their living by
writing?*

When I started to get my novels published, somebody wisely said to
me: 'Don't jump off the cliff yet.' I think it was good advice and I've
passed it on to young writers many times. Until 1989, when my
novel *Restoration* found a large audience and began to be translated
across Europe and beyond, I had subsidised my novel writing with
other (mainly writing) activities such as journalism and I also had a
part-time teaching post at the University of East Anglia. Now, I've
given that up and feel, in retrospect, that it took up too much
energy and stole from my creative self, but I also feel grateful that it
was there for a while. I still enjoy doing work for radio and I have
started to write movies, which means that on good days I can
imagine a high-kicking old age entirely free from money grief.

ROSE TREMAIN *is the author of seven novels, including* Sacred Country,
The Colonel's Daughter *and* Restoration, *which was shortlisted for the
Booker Prize and won the* Sunday Express *Book of the Year Award. She has
taught on the University of East Anglia's MA in Creative Writing and was
listed as one of* Granta *magazine's Best of Young British Novelists in 1983.*

Fay Weldon

It depends what you mean by a writer. The word has changed its meaning. There are many more of us than there used to be, per head of population. Moreover, we have become politicised. We do not want to admit we can live in a garret on bread and cheese, because that is what publishers and TV companies will then expect us to do.

And then, do you mean writing as a career choice (that is, 'I want to be a writer') or as a vocational act? ('I want to write this particular novel/play/article/biography, and am in fact already doing so.') It depends whether you are talking about men writers, women writers, mother writers or father writers. Any statistic other than applied to all human beings, and concerned with remuneration, needs to be divided into these four categories before sense can be made of it.

Let me reply thus (without prejudice):

1. *How much do you think a writer needs to live on?*

A childless writer can live on the dole if he/she has to. Or could until now: but since direction of labour is being introduced under the welfare-to-work scheme, this avenue is, alas, soon to be closed off. Paper and pen is all that a writer needs as the tools of his/her trade, and the backs of lottery slips are freely available in many outlets. Pens can be purloined: a serious writer will happily sacrifice his personal dignity to his art. Kerouac wrote his first novel on a roll of paper.

2. *Do you think a serious writer can earn this sum by his writing, and if so, how?*

A writer who lives on the dole is not likely to earn much from his writing, if this matters to him/her. Money begets money. Confidence begets confidence. £500 a week keeps a person in moderate comfort and self-esteem from which the desire and capacity to keep earning is likely to flow; and the computer from crashing. And no, the advice must always be, don't give up your day job until the prospects of earning a livelihood from writing look good.

3. *If not, what do you think is the most suitable second occupation for him?*

Journalism, advertising, the senior ranks of the civil service, are appropriate alternative professions. Anything where the 'would-be writer' must first decipher, distinguish and then narrate onto the page the thoughts and emotions in his/her head will do. This is the basic task of the writer, after all: out of the head and onto the page! Only later will the quality of that thought and emotion begin to matter, but after publication it is of course too late. Advertising seems to me preferable to journalism. The journalist is trained never to be found out in a lie – to at least seem to stick to the truth – so the jump to fiction can be difficult. If the journalist tells lies he loses his job. If the novelist speaks the truth he is sued for libel. The writer out of advertising finds the leap from selling product to selling ideas comparatively easy.

4. *Do you think literature suffers from the diversion of a writer's energy into other employments or is enriched by it?*

There has to be both time to contemplate, and something to contemplate upon. All writers are different. Some are enriched by contact with the world, others are defeated by it. Some are spurred on by insecurity and flourish on anxiety, some need ivory towers, some enjoy a room full of other people's screen-savers and noise.

Employment – by which is meant, I suppose, one's forcible attendance in a place outside the home, and the obligatory turning of the thoughts to someone else's interests, *not* one's own, and the consequent companionship and conversation of unlikely others – could be seen to broaden the mind: or indeed, as with poor Kafka, to drive the writer to the page in desperation. Depends.

5. *Do you think the State or any other institution should do more for writers?*

The State should do more for writers, but funds should be allocated by panels of practising writers, never by arts administrators. Otherwise, a profound boredom ensues. Darkness falls from the air. Takes a writer to know a writer, no matter how many creative writing modules the arts administrator has taken.

6. *Are you satisfied with your own solution of the problem and have you any specific advice to give to young people who wish to earn their living by writing?*

My own solution to the problem has been satisfactory enough, but I am lucky. When I began, what I wanted to write coincided with what people wanted to read. Advice to young people who want to be serious writers: if you have nothing to say, don't say it. Being young is a great disadvantage. Hang about, and time will cure the condition. If you write three chapters and then stop, you're not stuck, you're finished. What people say are your weak points may really be your strength – don't brake, go into the skid. And don't take any notice at all of anyone's advice.

FAY WELDON *is the author of twenty-two novels, including* The Life and Loves of a She-Devil, The Cloning of Joanna May *and, most recently,* Big Women. *She has also published four short-story collections, two children's books and three works of non-fiction, and has written over twenty major television plays, as well as innumerable radio and theatre plays.*

Hugo Williams

1. *How much do you think a writer needs to live on?*

I don't know about anyone else but now I've paid off my mortgage I
need about £12,000 for a reasonable life in London. I have to work
every day of the week to make that, although I don't work very hard.
It's the price of staying home.

2. *Do you think a serious writer can earn this sum by his writing, and if
so, how?*

Difficult to make enough to live on when you're starting out. The
National Assistance Board and Supplementary Benefit used to be
much more easy-going than the current Job Clubs and Welfare to
Work seem to be and I had many years of quiet subsidy off them
with no questions asked, for which I am grateful. 'Supplementary'
was a good word for it. I had my pension in advance, so I'm not too
cut up about its probable absconcion in the years to come. Yet.

   My policy was always to accept every last offer of work, no matter
how mad. Turning down stuff felt unlucky. But this scavenging life
depends on living in London and being amenable and shameless.

3. *If not, what do you think is the most suitable second occupation for him?*

The classic urban poet scrounger such as myself puts together his
wages from reviewing, creative writing, teaching, judging, readings,
poems, grants, mini-cab driving and shop-lifting, but I didn't

achieve this until I was nearly forty. A more dignified solution would be a carpenter, waiter or airline pilot, anything where you didn't have to bring work home. My own happier, better life will always be acting, but then everyone needs a road not taken to blame from time to time.

4. *Do you think literature suffers from the diversion of a writer's energy into other employments or is enriched by it?*

I'm sure I could have written more poems with less hack work to do, but is quantity important? I think it is. Practice makes better. Certainly there's nothing much you can do about the quality. I think I would never have tried prose at all without the financial spur and this has taken me to some interesting places where poems have resulted as well as cash and fun.

5. *Do you think the State or any other institution should do more for writers?*

Yes for me, no for everyone else. Which I take to be everyone's answer, really. In other words no. The question meant something in 1946, but today young writers are almost by definition award winners. I certainly had my whack, for doing practically nothing.

6. *Are you satisfied with your own solution of the problem and have you any specific advice to give to young people who wish to earn their living by writing?*

My own 'solution' took twenty years, 20–40, to impose itself on my expectations, like it or not. I wouldn't wish it on anyone who tends towards anxiety, let alone a hedonistic lifestyle, although film reviewing and column writing can be quite leisurely if you can get down to them. Far better be a tree surgeon, banker or marine biologist. That way the literary world will think you are a natural and award you special status. My other advice would be always write for one person, not a public. I remember writing something about a stupid master under the desk at school. It was exciting. Whatever feels illegal is likely to be where good writing originates.

A poet, critic and journalist, Hugo Williams has published one book of poems every five years since 1965, as well as a travel book (No Particular Place to Go) *and* Freelancing, *a collection of his writing for the* Times Literary Supplement. *A former television critic and poetry editor for the* New Statesman, *he has also been theatre critic for the* Sunday Correspondent *and film critic for* Harper's and Queen. *His most recent collection of poetry,* Dock Leaves *(1994), was selected as a Poetry Book Society Choice.*

1946

John Betjeman

1. *How much do you think a writer needs to live on?*

As much as anyone else.

2. *Do you think a serious writer can earn this sum by his writing, and if so, how?*

No person requiring intoxicating drinks, cigarettes, visits to cinemas and theatre and food above British Restaurant standard can afford to live by writing prose if he is not 'established'. Not even a popular poet, if there is one, can live by his poetry.

3. *If not, what do you think is the most suitable second occupation for him?*

I can speak only for myself. I would like to be a station-master on a small country branch line (single track).

4. *Do you think literature suffers from the diversion of a writer's energy into other employments or is enriched by it?*

I do not know.

5. *Do you think the State or any other institution should do more for writers?*

The State cannot possibly help a creative writer since, properly viewed, a writer is as much part of the State as a Civil Servant. You

are therefore asking should a writer do more for himself? A
Government Office certainly cannot help since it is concerned, or
should be concerned, with making living conditions tolerable, with
giving us enough to eat, proper roads and drains and heat and light
and arranging wars for us when our existence is threatened from
outside. A few writers find their inspiration in writing about politics
– most of them write vilely – but I would have thought the subject-
matter of a writer is irrelevant to this question. I do not see why
writers, as much as school-teachers or manual workers, should not
be entitled to a State pension when their powers are over. As it is,
they are subject to the publicity and niggardliness of the Civil List. A
decent pension should be the limit of help from a Government
Office.

The Society of Authors might arrange that when the State
approaches a writer to write something, the State should offer a fee
commensurate with a generous periodical instead of apologising for
the lowness of the fee and excusing it on the grounds that it is
Government work.

6. *Are you satisfied with your own solution of the problem and have you any
specific advice to give to young people who wish to earn their living by
writing?*

No. Who is? But if someone is born to be a writer nothing will
prevent his writing. Perhaps the bitter tests of today are a good
thing. But you need great strength of character. At all costs avoid an
advertising agency where you will either have to write lies or
embellish facts in which you are not interested; such work is of the
devil. Journalism is a better way out for weak characters, such as I
am, who are slaves to nicotine and drink. It teaches you to write
shortly and clearly. It allows you to say what you think – at least
reputable journalism does. It forbids you to be a bore.

But because I believe that there is such a thing as a balance
between mental work and manual work and because I believe that
in Britain today people are subjected to too much of one or too

much of the other, I would advise a young writer to equip himself for manual work which he thinks he will enjoy. It is pretty certain to be better paid than is writing in its initial stages. If I had my life over again, I think I would take up some handicraft – making stained glass or weaving or french polishing or woodcarving – and with this to fall back on and to content the manual side of me without destroying my soul, I would be refreshed and confident when I wrote. But I would have taken on such work with writing as my chief aim. I would have taken it on in self-defence because I knew I must write and that God had called me to be a writer, but demanded that I do my quota of work with my hands.

SIR JOHN BETJEMAN *was one of Britain's most popular twentieth-century poets. Poet Laureate from 1972, he published numerous collections of verse, including, before 1946,* Mount Zion *(1931),* Continual Dew: a little book of bourgeois verse *(1937) and* New Bats in Old Belfries *(1945). Probably his most famous work was* Summoned by Bells *(1960), a blank-verse autobiography. He died in 1984.*

Elizabeth Bowen

1. *How much do you think a writer needs to live on?*

I should say that, as in the case of any other kind of person, this depends on his liabilities and his temperament. In my own case, I should like to have £3,500 a year net.

2. *Do you think a serious writer can earn this sum by his writing, and if so, how?*

I should say that, with all past books in print and steady production still going on, a writer, if his or her name is still of value, should be able to command two-thirds of the sum I have named by the time he or she is 60 or 65.

3. *If not, what do you think is the most suitable second occupation for him?*

I should say in a man's case a suitable occupation would be either medicine, architecture or law. Very few women would have time to carry on two professions simultaneously as their personal life and domestic responsibilities take up a good deal of time in themselves.

4. *Do you think literature suffers from the diversion of a writer's energy into other employments or is enriched by it?*

I should think that a writer's writing would be improved by any activity that brought him into company with other than that of his fellow writers. Literary sequestration, which seems to be increasing, is most unfortunate. On the other hand, the diversion of energy is a danger. If a writer is doing two things at the same time he is likely to have more to write about, but runs the risk of writing with less high concentration and singleness of mind.

5. *Do you think the State or any other institution should do more for writers?*

I find this difficult to answer, as I am not clear how much the State does already. Writers who have worked hard and shown distinction (in any field, or of any kind) should certainly be entitled to some help, or even a degree of support, in the case of illness or old age. And, equally, some sense of responsibility should be felt by the public towards the dependents (young children, etc.) of such writers. As far as I know, an extension of the Literary Fund, and possibly a contribution to this from the State, should meet the purpose.

6. *Are you satisfied with your own solution of the problem and have you any specific advice to give to young people who wish to earn their living by writing?*

I doubt if one ever does arrive at a specific solution of the problem – it is a matter of getting along from year to year. My advice to young people who wish to earn their living by writing would be to go at it slowly, with infinite trouble, not burn any boats in the way of other support behind them, and not either expect or play for quick returns.

Born in 1899, ELIZABETH BOWEN *was an Anglo-Irish novelist and short story writer. Known for her skilful descriptions of landscapes and the nuances of upper and middle-class social life, she is best remembered for two novels,* The Death of the Heart *(1938) and* The Heat of the Day *(1949). She died in 1973.*

Alex Comfort

1. *How much do you think a writer needs to live on?*

I cannot lay down an income scale for 'writers', as if they were a race apart from anyone else. I live on a combined income of about £500 per annum, with a wife, and one child expected.

2. *Do you think a serious writer can earn this sum by his writing, and if so, how?*

In other words, can a writer who conscientiously produces work he considers artistically worth while live on the proceeds of it? Yes, obviously he can, if he happens to write in one of the genres or styles which are commercially subsidised, but in the present world it seems to me highly inadvisable for him to do so. It means that one has to impose some sort of quota in order to live comfortably; it renders one dependent on the phases of an opinion which one ought to be forming, not obeying, and it continually dangles the temptation of subsidy-conditional-on-conforming under one's nose. I would not try to live entirely upon literary work myself, even though at the moment I probably could get paid for everything I write without being obliged to alter it. The writers who are working experimentally, or in forms such as lyrical poetry, would be quite unable to live out of their work, if only because of the relatively small volume which can be produced by one man. I have no sympathy with the Chatterton-Rimbaud fairy stories which lead writers to starve in garrets, or, the more modern equivalent, sponge on non-literary friends, because they are poets and find work too mundane. Artists are not privileged people – art is probably the human activity most deeply dependent on a responsible attitude to other people.

3. *If not, what do you think is the most suitable second occupation for him?*

This depends upon the attitude which you adopt towards life. I believe that the most consistent and factually justifiable attitude towards life and art is Romanticism, by which I mean a philosophy based upon two postulates – that Man individually and collectively is engaged in continual conflict to assert the standards, beauty, justice, and so on, which are the product of his own consciousness against an inert universe and a hostile environment, on the one hand, and power on the other: and that by reason of this conflict we have a definite, inescapable duty and responsibility towards all other human beings. We are afloat on a raft in a sea of mindlessness – our cargo includes all the things which consciousness regards as valuable, and there are one or two people on board who have lost their heads and are busier trying to assert their own authority than working to keep the raft afloat. We have to fight them with one hand and the elements with the other. The two fights are part of one single conflict, and for me art is the name we give to the struggle for spiritual survival and science (the genuine article, not the kitsch variety) the fight against death and our environment. One can add revolution, the fight against the human allies of the dead environment. That is why I regard scientific activity as fully continuous with artistic activity – I don't know where one stops and the next starts. I do not suggest that all artists should try to become research workers, but I think that their second occupation should be one which bears some relation to the general effort of Man, which I call mutual aid.

4. *Do you think literature suffers from the diversion of a writer's energy into other employments or is enriched by it?*

5. *Do you think the State or any other institution should do more for writers?*

My answers follow from what I have said. Non-literary activity always enriches creation subject to my provisos. As to the State, since one of the major battles of the sane man in the present period is against obedience, an enemy second only to death, I don't think the artist should touch the State or its money with a barge-pole. The same applies to commercial patronage, increasingly, from day to day. In a period of barbarism one has to be able to cut oneself off from all patronage – put yourself in the place of the European underground writers, and remember that the responsible human being is a member of a permanent underground movement who must be ready to carry on his work in the devastated landscape of the next hundred years.

6. *Are you satisfied with your own solution of the problem and have you any specific advice to give to young people who wish to earn their living by writing?*

Yes, entirely satisfied. What I have written here and elsewhere about this question is the only advice I have to offer. It boils down to this – be human, fight death and obedience, work like anyone else, since that is part of humanness, despise kiss-breeches and collaborators, and produce the work which you feel compatible with these ideas.

For your information, my own non-literary posts at the moment are M.O. in a Borough Children's clinic and research assistant at a hospital. I am paid for the first, but not the second.

A poet, novelist and non-fiction writer, ALEX COMFORT *is the author of forty-two different books, including ten works of poetry, ten works of fiction and the bestselling* Joy of Sex *sequence.*

Cyril Connolly

1. *How much do you think a writer needs to live on?*

If he is to enjoy leisure and privacy, marry, buy books, travel and entertain friends, a writer needs upwards of five pounds a day net. If he is prepared to die young of syphilis for the sake of an adjective he can make do on under.

2. *Do you think a serious writer can earn this sum by his writing, and if so, how?*

He can only earn the larger sum if he writes a novel, play, or short story, which is bought by Hollywood and/or chosen by one of the American book societies, but he can add considerably to his income if he tries to publish everything he writes simultaneously in American periodicals, who all pay most handsomely. This is the only dignified way of making more money without giving up more time.

3. *If not, what do you think is the most suitable second occupation for him?*

A rich wife.

4. *Do you think literature suffers from the diversion of a writer's energy into other employments or is enriched by it?*

If you substitute 'painting' for 'literature', it becomes obvious that

no art can be enriched by the diversion of an artist's energy. A good
book is the end-product of an obsession; everything which impedes
the growth and final exorcism of this obsession is harmful. All
writers like to have hobbies and side interests to fill up the interval
between obsessions, but this is not the same as having other
employment. Compare Pope with Gray, Tennyson and Arnold,
Baudelaire with Merimée, Yeats with Houseman. Pope and Yeats
grew, the two dons, despite their long holidays, remained stationary.

5. *Do you think the State or any other institution should do more for writers?*

The State, in so far as it supplants private enterprise, must supplant
private patronage. But private patronage was not based on results,
and the State should not count on them either. Free gifts of money
should be made to those setting out on an artistic career, and at
intervals of seven years, to those who persist in one. Most of our
good writers need at the moment a year's holiday with pay.
Furthermore, pensions to artists and their widows should be trebled,
both in value and quantity, and considered an honour, not a
disgrace. All State-conferred honours to artists should be accom-
panied by a cash award. Furthermore, all writers and painters
should be allowed a fairly large entertainment allowance, free of tax,
and one annual tax-free trip abroad. Books and framed paintings
(as opposed to articles, sketches, posters etc.) should be regarded as
capital and the income from them not taxed. This would encourage
the production of books rather than the better-paid journalism by
which most writers now make their living. Money spent on buying
books and works of art by living artists should also be tax-free. Big
Business too, could do much more for writers and painters. Shell
and London Transport before the war were setting the example.
Even the general public can send fruit and eggs. The State's attitude
towards the artist should be to provide *luxe, calme et volupté*, and
when it receives *ordre et beauté* in return, to be sure to recognise it.

6. *Are you satisfied with your own solution of the problem and have you any specific advice to give to young people who wish to earn their living by writing?*

No, certainly not. What a question! As for the young, don't become writers unless you feel you must, and unless you can contemplate the happiness, security and cosiness of respectable State-employed people without loneliness or envy. Otherwise, like most of us, you will resemble the American 'who wanted to be a poet and ended up as a man with seven jobs'.

Instigator of the original 'Cost of Letters' questionnaire in 1946, Cyril Connolly was editor of the literary magazine Horizon *from its founding in 1939 to its close in 1950. The author of one novel –* The Rock Pool *(1936) – and two works of non-fiction –* Enemies of Promise *(1938) and* The Unquiet Grave *(1944) – as well as several collections of essays, he died in 1974.*

C. Day Lewis

1. *How much do you think a writer needs to live on?*
2. *Do you think a serious writer can earn this sum by his writing, and if so, how?*
3. *If not, what do you think is the most suitable second occupation for him?*
4. *Do you think literature suffers from the diversion of a writer's energy into other employments or is enriched by it?*
5. *Do you think the State or any other institution should do more for writers?*
6. *Are you satisfied with your own solution of the problem and have you any specific advice to give to young people who wish to earn their living by writing?*

I could not generalise about any of these questions. Ideal thing, for most writers: a private income – small enough not to encourage laziness or dilettantism, large enough to relieve the worries, obsessions and grosser expedients of poverty, say £150 to £300 a year. Failing this, should a young writer make his basic income from (a) literary hack-work, or (b) a second occupation? Depends so much upon the individual. Advantage of (a) is that it has (or can have) some relation to his serious work, something to do with words and ideas and even with the imagination; and one only learns how to write by writing – and 'hack' writing has its discipline, its opportunities to shirk, to twist, or to be honest and careful, just as does 'serious' writing: serious writing, in one sense, is any writing you take seriously. Advantage of (b), for the beginner at any rate, is that it is the best way for him to find out whether he is really meant to be a writer: if he is not, the interest of the second occupation will soon overshadow the interest of writing; and he will have made a start with this other profession, instead of having to start again from scratch. The most suitable second occupation for a serious writer? A routine job, with regular hours, spare time, and (particularly if he is a novelist) one which brings him much into contact with people: for the novelist, who needs a wide range and diversity of personal contacts, medicine, the law, or commercial travelling might be recommended: for the poet, in so far as he needs a deeper, narrower experience, the instinctive kind of human relationship which comes from working with other people is perhaps best – the relationship of a Civil Servant, a schoolmaster, or for that matter a soldier or a miner, with his colleagues. The poet is a special case, anyway: other serious writers can, with luck, and without loss of integrity, make a living from their writing when established; the poet cannot, by his poetry alone. Ideally, he should arrange his life more regularly than the novelist; there is a systole and diastole in his creative workings, and his life should be adapted to these – a period of taking in followed by a period of giving out. He, if any writer, should receive support from the State; for, on the whole, his writing will be apt to suffer more than others' from diversion of his energy either into hack writing or a second employment: but State support should involve him in no obligations except to his poetry; therefore it would best come from some non-political organisation such as the Arts Council. On the other hand, since friction stimulates, no writer should have things made too easy for him, materially, morally, psychologically: a smooth, cosy life in the bosom of the State, or the intelligentsia, will not do: it is in his struggle with the ordinary business of living, even more than in his struggle with problems of technique, that the writer finds his own level of seriousness.

Born in 1904, C. DAY LEWIS began his literary life as a polemical left-wing poet . The author, under the pseudonym of Nicholas Blake, of some twenty detective novels, he turned in the mid-1930s from politics to more personal and pastoral subjects. He was Poet Laureate from 1968 to his death in 1972.

Robert Graves

1. *How much do you think a writer needs to live on?*
2. *Do you think a serious writer can earn this sum by his writing, and if so, how?*
3. *If not, what do you think is the most suitable second occupation for him?*

'Serious writer' was, I think, a term invented by the young experimental writers of the Twenties to distinguish themselves from the commercial, academic, and elder writers whom they lumped together as their common enemies. But if *Horizon* is using the word in a less provocative sense, it includes such different types as the modern novelist who writes for entertainment but not according to a commercially dictated formula, the literary historian, and the poet.

Novel writing is not an all-time job, and there is nothing against a novelist having a secondary profession if he does not happen to have inherited, or married, money. Fielding was a police magistrate, Trollope a post office official, and for contemporary instances consult *Who's Who*.

The literary historian requires whatever it needs to live in a University society with ready access to specialist libraries and specialist colleagues. The snag is the difficulty of getting a salaried post that does not involve so much routine teaching that he cannot get on with his real work.

To be a poet is a condition rather than a profession. He requires whatever it needs to be completely his own master. This need not involve great expense – W. H. Davies solved the problem by being a professional tramp.

4. Do you think literature suffers from the diversion of a writer's energy into other employments or is enriched by it?

This is too broad a question for me to attempt to answer here.

5. Do you think the State or any other institution should do more for writers?

Those who pay the piper call the tune. The State (or any State-sponsored institution) is a dangerous patron of literature.

6. Are you satisfied with your own solution of the problem and have you any specific advice to give to young people who wish to earn their living by writing?

Everyone has to solve the problem in his own way. First by deciding to what category of writers he belongs. Many begin as poets or experimental writers, and end as journalistic hacks. On leaving the Army after the last war but one, I took a vow of poetic independence which I have kept ever since. The only job I took and held for a few months was that of Professor of English literature at Cairo University, but I was my own master, had only one hour a week lecturing, and resigned as soon as difficulties arose with my French and Belgian colleagues. That was twenty years ago, and I have lived ever since by writing biography and historical novels: a profession which I find more easily reconcilable than most with being a poet. Shakespeare himself admitted the difficulty of a secondary profession in his sonnet about the dyer's hand; and to say that I am satisfied with my solution would be indecent – it would imply a greater satisfaction with my work than Shakespeare seems to have felt with his.

As for advice, if the young writer really wants it: never write anything that you do not really want to write for its own sake, whatever the fee is. And if you have made no critical discovery about life or literature that you feel so important that you must write it down, putting everything else aside, in the most direct and careful language of which you are capable, then you are not a serious writer. Apply for a job with a newspaper, an advertising agency or the B.B.C. But if you are a serious writer and have no money, then live on your friends, relations or wits, until you can collect a public large enough to support you. (That took me twelve years.) If you must take a job, find one wholly unconnected with writing, leave it as soon as you are proficient in it, and either live on your friends again or take another quite different one.

I cannot answer the question in terms of pounds, shillings and pence, because I live abroad and, anyhow, never keep accounts, and have a large family to support.

The author of many volumes of poetry and essays as well as fiction, biography and children's books, Robert Graves is probably most famous not for his poetry, but for his autobiography, Goodbye to All That *(1929), and two of his historical novels,* I, Claudius *and* Claudius the God *(both 1934). A long-time resident of Majorca, he was professor of poetry at Oxford from 1961 to 1966. He died in 1985.*

Robert Kee

1. *How much do you think a writer needs to live on?*
2. *Do you think a serious writer can earn this sum by his writing, and if so, how?*
3. *If not, what do you think is the most suitable second occupation for him?*
4. *Do you think literature suffers from the diversion of a writer's energy into other employments or is enriched by it?*
5. *Do you think the State or any other institution should do more for writers?*
6. *Are you satisfied with your own solution of the problem and have you any specific advice to give to young people who wish to earn their living by writing?*

There is something inside all artists which remains themselves whatever happens, and this has nothing to do with income unless income is so low that they have neither time nor energy to be themselves.

The trouble is that few writers can be certain of obtaining regularly from their writings even the £400 a year which I regard as necessary to supply the time and energy with which to write. They have to turn to bureaucracy or journalism or some other activity which demands allegiance to society and thereby castrates them as writers. However, if there is no other way for a writer to get his £400 a year, a part-time extra job is at least preferable to a full-time one. And as a writer's business is to do with words it is obviously more sensible for him to turn to some form of word-using rather than to glass-blowing or road-making. But let him be quite clear about what he is doing. There should be no attempt to compromise between money-earning and writing. There are already too many writers who, in the higher forms of intellectual and literary journalism, have lost sight of their real work. The principle should be: the easier the money, the more suitable the second occupation. If a writer cannot find enough to write about in what goes on all round him, without being 'enriched' by other employments, he might as well give up being a writer altogether.

But the idea of a writer having to descend to tricks to be able to follow his trade is unpleasant, and the society which tolerates it is being short sighted merely because it means that so much less serious writing will be done. How then is a writer to get his £400 a year? I suppose publishers could be made to surrender a great deal more of it than they do at the moment. The present relationship between writer and publisher seems as absurd as if a man were to be paid pocket-money by his butler. But this is really irrelevant because even if publishers did pay fairly it would not help the writer who produces little or who is not in sympathy with his time.

Therefore the State, as the instrument of society, should make £400 a year available to anyone who wants to be a writer. This would be renewable every year at the option of the writer. The only condition would be that no other employment could be taken during that year. There would be few abuses of this system. £400 a year is not enough to tempt the crook. Moreover, any charlatan who had no intention of writing would get so bored with nothing to do on so little money that he would be eager to escape at the end of the year. Admittedly some appalling writers would be given a chance but, regarded as experimental waste, this would be a minor drawback. We are prepared to tolerate several million pounds-worth of experimental waste to produce a new atom bomb. Surely we could afford a few thousands to produce a new writer?

This £400 a year would in no way be an attempt to reward the writer for what he does. It would merely make it possible for him to write. The writer should be paid for what he is, not what he does. However, the State should also see that those writers who do produce something are more suitably rewarded than at present. No income tax should be payable on income derived from writing, though it would be payable on the basic £400. A considerable sum – say, the cost of about one afternoon at war – should be set aside every year to be distributed as prizes for poems, novels, criticism, editorship, etc. And if anyone thinks that this State interest in literature would lead to the same results as in the totalitarian countries, I would say that our literatures would resemble each other just about as much as our State legal systems do at present.

In answer to your last question I can only say I now enjoy £250 tax-free for one year on similar conditions to those which I have suggested. In so far as this is not £6 a week and will not continue after the end of the year, I am dissatisfied. In so far as it does give me a chance to write, I realise that I am more lucky than many writers who have already produced distinguished work.

ROBERT KEE *is the author of twelve books, including* A Crowd is Not Company, Trial and Error *and* The Green Flag, *a three-volume history of Ireland. A freelance journalist and broadcaster who has worked for many years on both radio and television, he is currently writing a biography of Mitterand.*

Laurie Lee

1. *How much do you think a writer needs to live on?*
2. *Do you think a serious writer can earn this sum by his writing, and if so, how?*
3. *If not, what do you think is the most suitable second occupation for him?*
4. *Do you think literature suffers from the diversion of a writer's energy into other employments or is enriched by it?*
5. *Do you think the State or any other institution should do more for writers?*
6. *Are you satisfied with your own solution of the problem and have you any specific advice to give to young people who wish to earn their living by writing?*

The commodity most necessary to the writer is not money at all, but time. The writer needs guaranteed time, long avenues of it stretching far away before him, free from congestion, side-tracks or concealed entrances. For ignoring the occasional lyric cartwheel, which covers no more than a moment of paper, serious writing is one of the most pedestrian occupations that exists.

I think few serious writers can earn this necessary time, legitimately, by the sort of writing they most wish to do. There are always the speed-kings, of course, but they pay heavily with blurred and half-seen images and phrases mutilated by the wind. A writer needs time to pause, to explore, to cultivate in detail the prospect before him. He needs to take time, and having taken it, to consume it in his own time.

But who among us is free to do this? Look at the panting cross-country novelists. Look at the six-day-bicycle-riding script writers, struggling at poems while changing tyres. Their doom is in the pace and the pay out; they are paid off by the number of milestones they cover, and not by their discoveries of the country in between. These are the things which break their hearts and wind.

Old-day patronage was in many ways evil, but at least it gave the artist time without tears. Its modern counterpart – State or commercial sponsorship in their present forms – is a great deal worse, for this, geared to the speed-neurosis of industry, induces in the writer all the jumping-jack hysteria of the factory-worker faced with the dictatorship of the moving belt.

What are the present alternatives? A he-man's job as wood-cutter or crane-driver, with a couple of hours writing in the evenings? Romantic fallacy! The body's exhaustion is also the mind's. A State job then – Ministry propagandist or B.B.C. hack? No; they fritter and stale like nobody's business.

What then? A State pension for all writers, with no questions asked? Not altogether; but that is more like it. Hardship and near-starvation are not bad for the young: they force the broader view, they stimulate, they atomise the coral-coasted island; they give birth to thoroughbreds of sublimation out of frustration. Let younger writers first serve this apprenticeship, and show something for it. Then, when they have passed the test, let the State provide them with sufficient pasture to live on, a free hand, and a bonus for special achievements. But do not let this be free altogether from the demands of commission. A fat pension, with no provisos, only encourages fatness; but extra sugar for spectacular leaps will keep the beasts in condition.

As to a present personal solution to the problem: my own serves me well enough, but I cannot say it would serve others. My rules are these: To avoid as far as possible the dissipation of regular work for others. Never to despise a commission unless I dislike it. Shelve any commission whenever the compulsion to do private work arises. But generally I welcome the rewards of scattered commissions; the discipline involved often provides channels for genuine personal expression. Anyway, I like writing for a waiting audience; and ever since my schooldays I have enjoyed making poems to a set subject. I only wish publishers and editors would issue that kind of challenge more often. Records are never broken except on a set course.

The author of a number of volumes of poetry, Laurie Lee is probably best-known for his works of autobiography, Cider with Rosie *(1959) and his two memoirs of the Spanish Civil War,* As I Walked Out One Midsummer Morning *(1969) and* A Moment of War *(1991). He died in 1997.*

Rose Macaulay

1. *How much do you think a writer needs to live on?*
2. *Do you think a serious writer can earn this sum by his writing, and if so, how?*
3. *If not, what do you think is the most suitable second occupation for him?*
4. *Do you think literature suffers from the diversion of a writer's energy into other employments or is enriched by it?*
5. *Do you think the State or any other institution should do more for writers?*
6. *Are you satisfied with your own solution of the problem and have you any specific advice to give to young people who wish to earn their living by writing?*

There can't be any general rule as to how much a writer needs to live on. But whatever it is, it is very unlikely that he will earn it at all early in his career, unless he happens to make a lucky hit, get chosen by book societies in this and other countries, perhaps even get filmed. The ordinary young writer, whether serious or not, must depend on something else for some years. If he (or she) has good-natured and moderately well-off parents, they may consent to keep him (or, more likely, her) till he finds his feet, or, alternatively, finds that he had better adopt another career. If the parents refuse this burden, as well they may, and if there are no other means of support, the young writer should enter some profession, the less exacting the better. If possible, he should choose a job that does not run counter to and stultify his creative instincts; either purely mechanical or physical work, whose hang-over would not impinge on his leisure, but which he could forget entirely when he laid down his tools each day and turned to his writing; or work that ministered to his imagination. It might be useful to get a job abroad for a time. Southey had a notion that he would be happy and fruitful if only he could get the consulship at Lisbon – 'Tis a good thousand a year' – though as a matter of fact the Lisbon consuls have always been busier than he supposed, and have had little time for literary pursuits. On the other hand, diplomats, whether ambassadors or holding some lesser post in a legation, have often written a great deal. Councillors and First Secretaries have been eloquent, and chancelleries have been nests of singing-birds or of experimenters in prose. But diplomacy, of course, is out of the reach of most young writers; it is a profession approached over stiff hurdles. Easier to be a tourist agent abroad (if you know any languages), or get a job in a café or a foreign bank or firm. That way, the writer will see life a little, which should be good for him. Much better not enter an intellectual profession, such as the law, medicine, or teaching, which will absorb his mind. In former times, the country parson's was often a life which gave scope for literature and scholarship; the fact that this is seldom now the case may indicate the decline of intellectual quality among clergymen. The number of our clerical authors in the past – and down almost to the present generation – is greater than in any other one profession; the quality of their work perhaps higher. However, if the writer succeeds in finding the job to suit him – preferably a series of jobs – his professional work should enrich his talent.

The State might well consider helping young writers with temporary maintenance. 'Let there be patrons,' as Herrick (himself patroned by Emmanuel Porter) urged in moving verse. Patrons have gone out; the State might do something to fill the gap. There might be a committee for the purpose of selecting worthy candidates. As no one can tell at first whether a serious writer is a bad serious writer or a good one, a few risks would have to be taken, and a few bad writers helped, as they were often helped by patrons of old. This does no great harm; better that than good young men and women should be forced to earn their daily bread by work that uses up all their energies and stultifies their talent. All the same, writers should be ready to live a little hard; to travel cheaply if at all, to eat and drink simply. They had better not be in a hurry to get married; this leads to expense, and, if they are young women, to devastating distraction of energy. (Unless, of course, they manage to marry money, which solves the problem at once.)

A popular satirical novelist of the 1920s and 1930s, as well as an accomplished essayist and travel writer, DAME ROSE MACAULAY *is best known for two works of fiction both published in the 1950s,* The World My Wilderness *(1950) and* The Towers of Trebizond *(1956). She died in 1958.*

J. Maclaren-Ross

1. *How much do you think a writer needs to live on?*
2. *Do you think a serious writer can earn this sum by his writing, and if so, how?*
3. *If not, what do you think is the most suitable second occupation for him?*
4. *Do you think literature suffers from the diversion of a writer's energy into other employments or is enriched by it?*
5. *Do you think the State or any other institution should do more for writers?*

6. *Are you satisfied with your own solution of the problem and have you any specific advice to give to young people who wish to earn their living by writing?*

Your questionnaire arrived at an opportune moment, when I was at my wits end to know which way to turn for money. This situation is always arising with me. Hence, my answer to your first question is: A writer needs all he can lay his hands on in order to keep alive.

How much he actually should have depends on the writer himself: his tastes and habits. In other words, he should be able to live comfortably, in a style that suits his temperament. If he is a drinker he shouldn't have to worry whether he drinks beer or spirits or wine, though he shouldn't necessarily have enough to get sozzled every night. If he is a smoker he shouldn't have to buy Woodbines if he prefers Perfectos. If he wants to buy a book he should be able to buy it, not wait until it is sent to him for review or lent to him by a friend. If he doesn't drink, smoke, read books or go to the cinema, then he almost certainly has other vices, or else a wife or mistress to spend money on; well, he should have enough to spend. A writer's standard of living should be at the least as high as that of a solicitor, or any other professional man.

I am a metropolitan man and I need a minimum of £20 a week to live on, given the present cost of living; and that's not including rent. Whether I get it or not is another matter.

Which brings me to your second question: How can a serious writer earn this sum by writing? It's very difficult. Suppose, like myself at the moment, you have written short stories but now want to write novels. How do you raise the sum of money needed to sit down and concentrate on writing a novel in moderate peace of mind? You can't do it except by more short stories, radio plays, or what have you, the writing of which takes up most of your time and vitiates your energy. So the novel doesn't get written, that's all.

Suppose, however, you are fortunate enough to obtain an advance of £300, you certainly spend more than that while writing the book, so you're no better off; in these days of small editions and reprints at long intervals, your advance almost covers the total royalties on your sales. Then there is the interval between delivery of manuscript, and the appearance of the book: nine months to a year if you are lucky, three years if you are not, as in one case I know. After that there is a further period until statements of sales go through and royalties are paid up; any attempt to obtain money in between is regarded by the publisher as an imposition, or, if he doles out some small sum, as an act of charity.

Besides, advances are rarely anything like £300. They are more likely to be, at the most, £75 or £100. *The Artists' and Writers' Year Book* is still talking about £25 as a suitable advance, 'but only in rare cases can publishers be made to see this'.

Therefore, a novelist is supposed to spend six months writing his book and then live for a further eighteen months or so on his advance – about £100. Plainly impossible, with present cost of living, even for a man of the most spartan tastes.

Publishers should be made to acknowledge the higher cost of living and to pay advances in proportion; a minimum of £300 should be forced upon them, and even that will not keep anyone for eighteen months. The rates paid by editors for poems, articles, stories, are far higher now than they were before the war. Why haven't publishers raised their rates accordingly?

Until they do, the writer is compelled to exist by means, in my opinion, detrimental to his serious work. In many occupations, like film-script writing, the B.B.C. etc., he has neither the leisure nor the energy, when the day's dull work is done, to settle to what he really wants to do. I don't think there can possibly be any occupations suitable to the writer other than that of writing what he wants when he wants and of being well paid for doing so.

I don't think, either, that the State or any other institution should support writers. Such a state of affairs would inevitably lead to limitation or control of subject-matter and theme. It is the publishers and editors, who make money and reputation out of printing writers, who should do more for the people on whose work they in turn depend for their living.

But this solution to the problem does not satisfy me, since I see no hope of the present vicious system being altered; and if I have advice to give to anyone who wants to write for a living, it is this:

(a) Don't attempt it.

(b) If you are crazy enough to try, be tough; get all you can. Price your work high and make them pay. Don't listen to your publisher's sob-stories about how little he can afford. He'll have a country house and polo ponies when you are still borrowing the price of a drink in Fitzrovia. Remember, he makes the money; make him give you as much as you can extort, short of using a gun or pincers. Art for art's sake is all cock, anyway.

And by the same token, please pay promptly for this contribution, because I am broke.

A former vacuum-cleaner salesman, JULIAN MACLAREN-ROSS *was the most elegant and raffish member of wartime Bohemia. He made his name as a writer with* The Stuff to Give the Troops, *but is best remembered for his posthumously published* Memoirs of the Forties.

George Orwell

1. *How much do you think a writer needs to live on?*

At the present purchasing value of money, I think £10 a week after payment of income tax is a minimum for a married man, and perhaps £6 a week for an unmarried man. The best income for a writer, I should say – again at the present value of money – is about £1,000 a year. With that he can live in reasonable comfort, free from duns and the necessity to do hackwork, without having the feeling that he has definitely moved into the privileged class. I do not think one can with justice expect a writer to do his best on a working-class income. His first necessity, just as indispensable to him as are tools to a carpenter, is a comfortable, well-warmed room where he can be sure of not being interrupted; and although this does not sound much, if one works out what it means in terms of domestic arrangements, it implies fairly large earnings. A writer's work is done at home, and if he lets it happen he will be subjected to almost constant interruption. To be protected against interruption always costs money, directly or indirectly. Then again, writers need books and periodicals in great numbers, they need space and furniture for filing papers, they spend a great deal on correspondence, they need at any rate part-time secretarial help, and most of them probably benefit by travelling, by living in what they consider sympathetic surroundings, and by eating and drinking the things they like best and by being able to take their friends out to meals or have them to stay. It all costs money. Ideally I would like to see every human being have the same income, provided that it were a fairly high income:

but so long as there is to be differentiation, I think the writer's place is in the middle bracket, which means, at present standards, round about £1,000 a year.

2. *Do you think a serious writer can earn this sum by his writing, and if so, how?*

No, I am told that at most a few hundred people in Great Britain earn their living solely by writing books, and most of those are probably writers of detective stories, etc. In a way it is easier for people like Ethel M. Dell to avoid prostitution than it is for a serious writer.

3. *If not, what do you think is the most suitable second occupation for him?*

If it can be so arranged as not to take up the whole of his time, I think a writer's second occupation should be something non-literary. I suppose it would be better if it were also something congenial. But I can just imagine, for instance, a bank clerk or an insurance agent going home and doing serious work in his evenings; whereas the effort is too much to make if one has already squandered one's energies on semi-creative work such as teaching, broadcasting or composing propaganda for bodies such as the British Council.

4. *Do you think literature suffers from the diversion of a writer's energy into other employments or is enriched by it?*

Provided one's whole time and energies are not used up, I think it benefits. After all, one must make some sort of contact with the ordinary world. Otherwise, what is one to write about?

5. *Do you think the State or any other institution should do more for writers?*

The only thing the State could usefully do is to divert more of the

public money into buying books for the public libraries. If we are to
have full Socialism, then clearly the writer must be State-supported,
and ought to be placed among the better-paid groups. But so long
as we have an economy like the present one, in which there is a
great deal of State enterprise but also large areas of private
capitalism, then the less truck a writer has with the State, or any
other organised body, the better for him and his work. There are
invariably strings tied to any kind of organised patronage. On the
other hand, the old kind of private patronage, in which the writer is
in effect the dependent of some individual rich man, is obviously
undesirable. By far the best and least exacting patron is the big
public. Unfortunately the British public won't at present spend
money on books, although it reads more and more and its average
of taste, I should say, has risen greatly in the last twenty years. At
present I believe the average British citizen spends round about £1 a
year on books, whereas he spends getting on for £25 on tobacco and
alcohol combined. Via the rates and taxes he could easily be made
to spend more without even knowing it – as, during the war years, he
spent far more than usual on radio, owing to the subsidising of the
B.B.C. by the Treasury. If the Government could be induced simply
to earmark larger sums for the purchase of books, without in the
process taking over the whole book trade and turning it into a
propaganda machine, I think the writer's position would be eased
and literature might also benefit.

6. *Are you satisfied with your own solution of the problem and have you any
specific advice to give to young people who wish to earn their living by
writing?*

Personally I am satisfied, i.e. in a financial sense, because I have
been lucky, at any rate during the last few years. I had to struggle
desperately at the beginning, and if I had listened to what people
said to me I would never have been a writer. Even until quite
recently, whenever I have written anything which I took seriously,
there have been strenuous efforts, sometimes by quite influential

people, to keep it out of print. To a young writer who is conscious of having something in him, the only advice I can give is not to take advice. Financially, of course, there are tips I could give, but even those are of no use unless one has some kind of talent. If one simply wants to make a living by putting words on paper, then the B.B.C., the film companies, and the like are reasonably helpful. But if one wants to be primarily a writer, then, in our society, one is an animal that is tolerated but not encouraged – something rather like a house sparrow – and one gets on better if one realises one's position from the start.

Novelist, essayist, journalist and pamphleteer, GEORGE ORWELL *was the author, amongst other things, of two major works of polemic,* The Road to Wigan Pier *and* Homage to Catalonia, *and two of the century's most influential novels,* 1984 *and* Animal Farm. *He died in 1950.*

V. S. Pritchett

1. *How much do you think a writer needs to live on?*

Before the war I remember J. Middleton Murry held that a writer could honestly earn about £400 a year. Aldous Huxley estimated the need at about £700. The post-war equivalent would be about £1,200 to £1,400 gross.

2. *Do you think a serious writer can earn this sum by his writing, and if so, how?*

A vastly successful novelist, playwright, etc., can, of course, earn much more. But the promising, the rising, the merely successful, cannot earn anything like the above sums, by writing books or serious criticism or good short stories or poems, alone. The good creative writer will have to supplement his income from journalism, broadcasting, publishers' reading, editorial work, some other job – or a private income.

3. *If not, what do you think is the most suitable second occupation for him?*

Any secondary work.

4. *Do you think literature suffers from the diversion of a writer's energy into other employments or is enriched by it?*

But it is essential that it should take up very little time and energy.

This hardly ever happens, and the result is an evident decline in the quality of creative literature. The writers are worn out, overworked; they are not worn out by creation but by the various grindstones by which they earn the major part of their living. I would say that up to the age of thirty it does not matter what a writer does with his time. An outside job may be valuable. After thirty, the outside job is inevitable in our high-costing, highly taxed society, where the private income is vanishing – inevitable, and in the long run fatal.

5. *Do you think the State or any other institution should do more for writers?*

The question really amounts to this: should the State replace the support given by sinecures and the private income? No. State writers are bought and censored writers. I am against writers' co-operatives. I am in favour of the people who now have the large private fortunes being obliged, by the State, to support literature. These private fortunes are not in private hands. They are in the hands of the Boards, the shareholders of the great industrial firms. Shell-Mex, Unilever, London Transport, etc., should be obliged to give patronage – but not in return for publicity.

6. *Are you satisfied with your own solution of the problem and have you any specific advice to give to young people who wish to earn their living by writing?*

Advice to a young writer: discipline yourself to the habit of writing. Write every day. Keep office hours. Inspiration comes from the grindstone, not from heaven. Do not hope to move up from popular writing to more distinguished levels. Popular journalism corrupts very quickly. Write for yourself alone as long as you can; the conditions of the profession will gradually vitiate the highest standards. The failures of overwork are fewer than the failures of idleness. Move heaven and earth to get time, and put time before money whenever you can. Be born with a small private income; or get yourself supported by a husband or wife.

An accomplished novelist and critic, SIR V. S. PRITCHETT *is best known for his many short stories.* The Spanish Virgin and other stories *(1939) was the first of several collections, including* You Make Your Own Life *(1938) and* The Camberwell Beauty *(1974). The author of two autobiographical works,* The Cab at the Door *(1968) and* Midnight Oil *(1971), he died in 1996.*

Herbert Read

1. *How much do you think a writer needs to live on?*

How much a writer needs to live on will depend on his personal appetites, but if he is married, has two or three children, likes decent food and a comfortable house, he will need with present costs at least £1,000 a year.

2. *Do you think a serious writer can earn this sum by his writing, and if so, how?*

A serious writer cannot possibly earn this sum by writing. A serious book takes two or three years to write. To earn the necessary sum by book royalties, he would have to sell between thirty and fifty thousand copies of each book: in all probability he will sell only three to five thousand copies.

3. *If not, what do you think is the most suitable second occupation for him?*

The most suitable second occupation for him is one which is no drain on either his intellectual or physical energy. 'A nice job in a museum', jobs in publishers' offices and cultural organisations like the British Council and the B.B.C. are the worst possible kinds of occupation. They are too interesting: they overlap into his literary work. They create mental confusion and lead to all kinds of trivial activities which are intellectually exhausting and completely unremunerative.

Farming and small-holding, which have superficial attractions (especially for romantic writers) are physically far too exhausting. They drug the mental faculties with a poisonous fatigue.

The best kind of occupation is represented by Spinoza's lens-polishing. If I were beginning my life again, I should seek a job in the light engineering industry, especially one in which, by piece-work, the necessary amount of work could be varied according to the needs of the moment.

4. *Do you think literature suffers from the diversion of a writer's energy into other employments or is enriched by it?*

The more a writer has experience of the normal activities of human beings, the better it is for his writing. I can think of no great writer in the past who has not benefited from non-intellectual activities. I can think of many whose work has suffered from academic or hedonistic seclusion.

5. *Do you think the State or any other institution should do more for writers?*

No. The State can only demoralise and debase literature.

6. *Are you satisfied with your own solution of the problem and have you any specific advice to give to young people who wish to earn their living by writing?*

I am far from satisfied with my own solution of the problem. I have tried several solutions – Civil Servant, museum assistant, university professor, editor of a magazine, and now a publisher. They have all been unsatisfactory, for the reasons given in my answer to Question 3 above. They bristle with the 'grappling-irons' which Cézanne so rightly feared, and although a strong-minded individual might be able to avoid the public responsibilities which will eventually attach to eminence in such a position, nevertheless all such jobs are by their nature 'contact jobs', and whichever way one turns one meets the devouring pack – until in the end one is reduced to a condition of dazed indifference, the paralysis of the cornered animal.

My advice to young people who wish to earn their living by writing is at all costs to avoid following my example.

SIR HERBERT READ, *father of the novelist Piers Paul Read, was a prolific poet who was best known for his literary criticism and writing on art. As well as studies of, amongst others, Wordsworth and Malory, he wrote such texts as* The True Voice of Feeling *(1953),* Essays in Literary Criticism *(1969),* Art and Industry *(1934) and* Education through Art *(1943). He died in 1968.*

Stephen Spender

1. *How much do you think a writer needs to live on?*

Of course, what a writer needs depends on many things, such as his age, whether he is married, etc. The one impregnable position is readiness to make every economic sacrifice to his vocation and, if necessary, involve everyone round him in such sacrifice. But very few writers can do this. Allowing for travel and occasional treats, I should say an unmarried writer needs £500 or £600 a year (free of tax), if he lives in London. A married writer, if he makes his wife his cook, needs £700. However, if he has children, if he does not wish his wife to be a domestic slave and if he has any social life, he needs £1,000 a year or more.

Directly he needs as much as this, difficulties of income tax arise, for he needs actually to earn £1,500 a year. Writing is a social occupation and in London he will find that entertaining is one of his chief expenses. If he were a business man, the government would pay for his lunches with his colleagues, but as he is an artist, entertainment of other writers will not be recognised as a legitimate expense of his profession.

2. *Do you think a serious writer can earn this sum by his writing, and if so, how?*

Try to earn £1,000 a year or more from writing today and see what happens. If you write books your publisher will not have paper to print more than 5,000 copies, which will bring you in £250 to £350.

This means you must either write four to six books a year, or you must turn to journalism. Assuming you are paid, on the average, £3 3s. for 1,000 words, you will have to write 333,000 words a year to gain £1,000. Myself, I find that if I write three or four articles a week (a) I become irritable, (b) I get into a condition in which I find it very difficult to read seriously, (c) least of all can I read what I write myself. I can write an article far more easily than I can bear to read it, for the purpose of proof correcting, (d) there follows a general disgust with my own ideas, my way of thinking and talking, and (e) a tendency to write more and more journalism and less poetry, because I feel unworthy to write serious work.

3. *If not, what do you think is the most suitable second occupation for him?*

I can only state the problems in general terms. These are (a) to avoid expressing merely in words on a level which lowers one's standards, (b) to avoid exhausting oneself physically and/or mentally, (c) to avoid becoming absorbed in some task which eventually becomes more important to one than one's writing, (d) to avoid being forced to play some role in life – such as an official or a pedagogue or an important person – which usurps one's creative personality.

The safest part for a writer to play in a job is a return to childhood. Do some job which enables one to learn something which will be useful in writing.

Accept the fact that one is once again the stupidest boy in the class, the backward son in the family. One's best relationship with one's colleagues is for them to think of one as slightly mad but full of good will. Be a cog and allow oneself to be gently ground between the heads of departments. Reassure people by allowing them to think that one is distinguished without one's ever menacing their own position. For God's sake never be in a position of responsibility and have no ambitions. Do not seek honours and do not refuse them. One should aim at being a rather superior and privileged office clown who excites no one's envy, and on whom one's colleagues project a few fantasies. One encourages all this by arriving always a little late (but not too late). Prepare for the worst, when the boss shows you his (or his wife's or his son's) poems. Pretend to like them, ask for a testimonial and resign immediately when this happens.

4. *Do you think literature suffers from the diversion of a writer's energy into other employments or is enriched by it?*

This depends entirely on the quantity of the writer's energy. If he has the energy to do another job and to write, I cannot help thinking that his writing gains by a contact with the machinery of ordinary life. A scientist, a managerial leader or a statesman who realises an idea which has to pass through the whole machinery of modern organisation, is creative in a way parallel to an artist who overcomes technical problems in order to state an idea in his particular medium. If one can retain the sense of a creative attitude in one's environment and not be crushed by a routine, one will learn much from ordinary work. Myself, I think that the best and most serious modern literature suffers from unworldliness. Literature should be made of the same worldly muck as are the historic plays of Shakespeare, the courtly drama of Racine and of Lopez de Vega, the materialistic novels of Balzac and the Duchy of Parma in *La Chartreuse de Parme.* Byron was the last worldly poet. What we want is a fusion of Byron and Blake.

5. *Do you think the State or any other institution should do more for writers?*

Only in the way of recognising and protecting the writer's professional position, by providing paper for modern books, giving creative writers the travel facilities of journalists, allowing the social contacts of writers with their colleagues to count as tax-free business expenses, etc.

6. *Are you satisfied with your own solution of the problem and have you any specific advice to give to young people who wish to earn their living by writing?*

At the moment I am happy because I work with an intelligent and sympathetic international group of people who, not being English, expect of me what I can give, do not make me feel guilty and have an unobtrusive recognition of my value in their work and also in my own which has a certain value for them. I am not unpatriotic, but I fear that the mainspring of English industriousness is a sense of guilt and for this reason the position of writers who have to work for their living in this country is particularly difficult. They are forced into the dilemma of feeling they have to choose between two kinds of work. In France, this is not so, with the result that many French writers combine official positions with writing.

I advise the young writer to be perfectly honest with himself about the all-important problem of how he is expending his energy. The only rule in this work is to know what you want to do and do it, at all costs. If you can do other things as well, you will probably gain by it. But if you can't, you're *foútu*.

Co-founder of Horizon *with Cyril Connolly,* SIR STEPHEN SPENDER *was closely associated with the poets W.H. Auden and Christopher Isherwood in the 1930s. The author of several critical studies as well as many volumes of poetry, he died in 1997.*

Dylan Thomas

1. *How much do you think a writer needs to live on?*

He needs as much money as he wants to spend. It is after his housing, his feeding, his warming, his clothing, the nursing and looking after his children, etc., have been seen to – and these should be seen to by the State – that he really needs money to spend on all the luxurious necessities. Or, it is then that he doesn't need money because he can do without those necessary luxuries. How much money depends, quite obviously, on how much he wants to buy. I want a lot, but whether I need what I want is another question.

2. *Do you think a serious writer can earn this sum by his writing, and if so, how?*

A serious writer (I suppose by this you mean a good writer, who might be comic) can earn enough money by writing seriously, or comically, if his appetites, social and sensual, are very small. If these appetites are big or biggish, he cannot earn, by writing what he wishes to write, enough to satisfy them. So he has to earn money in another way: by writing what he doesn't want to write, or by having quite another job.

3. *If not, what do you think is the most suitable second occupation for him?*

It's no good, I suppose, saying that I know a couple of good writers who are happy writing, for a living, what they don't particularly want to write, and also a few good writers who are happy (always qualified by words I'm not going to use now) being bank clerks, civil servants, etc. I can't say how a writer can make money most suitably. It depends on how much money he wants and on how much he wants it and on what he is willing to do to get it. I myself get about a quarter of the money I want by writing what I don't want to write and at the same time trying to, and often succeeding in, enjoying it. Shadily living by one's literary wits is as good a way of making too little money as any other, so long as, all the time you are writing B.B.C. and film scripts, reviews, etc., you aren't thinking, sincerely, that this work is depriving the world of a great poem or a great story. Great, or at any rate very good, poems and stories do get written in spite of the fact that the writers of them spend much of their waking time doing entirely different things. And even a poet like Yeats, who was made by patronage financially safe so that he need write and think nothing but poetry, had voluntarily to give himself a secondary job: that of philosopher, mystic, crank, quack.

4. *Do you think literature suffers from the diversion of a writer's energy into other employments or is enriched by it?*

No, to both questions. It neither suffers nor is it enriched. Poems, for instance, are pieces of hard craftsmanship made interesting to craftsmen in the same job, by the work put into them, and made interesting to everybody, which includes those craftsmen, by divine accidents: however taut, inevitably in order, a good poem may appear, it must be so constructed that it is wide open, at any second, to receive the accidental miracle which makes a work of craftsmanship a work of art.

5. *Do you think the State or any other institution should do more for writers?*

The State should do no more for writers than it should do for any other person who lives in it. The State should give shelter, food, warmth, etc., whether the person works for the State or not. Choice of work, and the money that comes from it should then be free for that man; what work, what money, is his own bother.

6. *Are you satisfied with your own solution of the problem and have you any specific advice to give to young people who wish to earn their living by writing?*

Yes and No, or vice versa. My advice to young people who wish to earn their living by writing is: DO.

Fêted both during his lifetime and after his early death at the age of 39, DYLAN THOMAS *was an exuberant and flamboyant poet whose romantic and rhetorical style found a huge audience on both sides of the Atlantic. Most famous for* Under Milk Wood *(1950), he died in America in 1953.*

Afterword

The Writer, the State and a Question of Attitude

by Gary McKeone

F. Scott Fitzgerald spent much of his creative life in financial peril. While Gatsby turned his West Egg mansion into a carnival of excess, Gatsby's creator lived in the stomach-tightening fear that the fictional world of wealth would be thrown into ironic relief by the actual world of hovering debt. The dry arithmetic of Fitzgerald's ledger is a cautionary tale and if the heavens have room for another patron saint of writers, a seat should be reserved for Fitzgerald's humane and generous editor, Maxwell Perkins.

Not a single word of Fitzgerald's fiction was written on state funding. He relied solely on income from his craft which he compromised again and again to write for high-paying magazines. When that particular furrow turned arid, he was forced to call on the kindness of friends. Scott Fitzgerald died on 21 December 1941. He had seven hundred dollars in cash. Six hundred and thirteen dollars went to the undertaker.

Talent revealed, talent compromised, financial security, financial hardship, public renown, the fall from favour; a lonely death on the margins of society. The cocktail has long since been shaken into literary legend but the ingredients are no less current today. Julian Barnes cites the case of a well-known 1960s novelist whose last Christmas dinner was provided by the Salvation Army.

At the 1997 Paul Hamlyn Awards for Writers, poet Adrian Mitchell revealed that the average annual income of the hundreds of poets who applied for one of the five awards was twelve thousand five hundred pounds. That was the average. Many were on less, far less, few on more. I know of small press publishers whose annual income is less than half that amount.

State funding for the arts is channelled primarily through the Arts Council. The government provides the money, the Arts Council sets policy. That policy is independent of government. Literature, traditionally and inexcusably the Cinderella of the arts funding system, attracts under one per cent of the annual allocation from the government. We use such limited resources to support writers through dedicated awards and by providing employment opportunities through live Literature events and residencies. We support publishers, literary magazines and translations; we support Literature in education, Literature in public libraries, Literature and broadcasting. We fund Literature organisations ranging from the Arvon Foundation to the Poetry Book Society, from Book Trust to the British Centre for Literary Translation. Every penny of the necessarily thinly spread budget is dedicated to the support of writing and reading.

The National Lottery has provided the wherewithal for some exceptional capital projects such as the Poetry Place in London and DARTS in Doncaster. *Arts for Everyone* has supported a clutch of projects which promote, among other initiatives, reading development, Literature festivals and writers' residencies. There has been a strong emphasis on engaging young people. I outline these areas so that readers can be clear about the work we already do in support of Literature.

Other organisations also help writers. Both the Authors Foundation and the Royal Society of Literature offer direct support to writers in financial need. This is important and valued work. Then, of course, there are the literary prizes, not to everyone's taste but with a part to play nonetheless.

Of course we could do more. There is always more to be done, more money needed. Support for the individual writer is clearly an area which must be addressed. Some of the regional Arts Boards are able to offer awards to writers within their area. The Arts Council currently offers nationally fifteen awards of seven thousand pounds each annually. This money is intended to buy time for a writer engaged on a work in progress. There are minimal conditions attached and the awards are made primarily by writers to writers. As Fay Weldon rightly points out, 'Takes a writer to know a writer, no matter how many creative writing modules the arts administrator has taken.'

If our commitment to supporting the individual writer is to mean anything, we must increase the number and value of such awards. This we can try to do via the capricious world of commercial sponsorship. Better still would be to persuade the government to take writers and writing seriously. Look at Ireland where *Aosdána* guarantees two hundred artists from all disciplines, chosen by their peers, five yearly emoluments. In the meantime, let's have a Writers Awards Trust Fund, enabling us to make fifty awards of fifteen thousand pounds per year. Let's have a government which takes writers and writing seriously enough to offer worthwhile tax exemption on advances and royalties. Let's have a government which values writers enough to offer a decent pension to those who have enhanced the cultural life of the nation.

Support for the writer is not, however, just about money. It is about a cultural attitude. We have to shift from what Salman Rushdie calls the 'culture of denigration' to the confident acknowledgement that, as Shena Mackay writes, a 'civilisation is judged by its art'. Literature is at the centre of that art.

Several of the writers who responded to the questionnaire worried about the *quid pro quo* of state assistance. It is a valid concern but this is not about some sort of malign intervention. Arts Council policy is independent of the government. This is about recognising the value of Literature to the cultural life of the country. It is, in Fred D'Aguiar's words, about 'ameliorating the conditions under which writers function'. That is as good a description of the Arts Council's role in Literature as any.

Of course, there are writers who believe that no public money should go directly to writers. Equally, there are writers like A. L.

Kennedy who look beyond the needs of the individual and urge the state to have 'a coherent arts policy which acknowledges the importance of the arts as an employer, as an index and guardian of our national well-being and as a source of communal and individual joy, encouragement and enlightenment.'

It would be the safe, bureaucratic thing to say that I can see both points of view. I cannot. If a nation is minded to support culture through public subsidy, Literature is part of that culture and writers are its impetus. Writers should be funded to write. We are talking about making the financial life of a writer as favourable as possible. Part of this will involve direct financial support. It will also involve tax incentives, pension arrangements, insurance, anything which registers on the personal balance sheet.

Several writers refer to the important and declining role of libraries. Public libraries have played a significant part in the lives of writers and readers. It was in Hackney Public Library that Harold Pinter discovered Joyce, Lawrence, Hemingway, Virginia Woolf and company. New York Public Library helped nurture the literary instincts of James Baldwin. Libraries are our Literature Centres. They are at the heart of almost every community and they are at the heart of the Arts Council's policy for Literature.

What does this mean in practical terms? It means that the Arts Council and the Regional Arts Boards have initiated projects which train librarians in Literature promotion. We have funded reader development projects. We have promoted writers events in libraries. There is more to be done. Library book-buying budgets are declining. This has to change. Contemporary Literature has to find its way onto the shelves if we are to keep the literary culture fresh. Read Michael Holroyd who puts the case succinctly: 'For a start the Secretary of State who has the responsibility to preserve and promote libraries should see to it that our libraries have a great deal more money to spend on books – that really would be "education, education, education" for us all. He should then increase the Public Lending Right by at least ten times.' An increased Public Lending Right helps authors.

The Arts Council does support writers and writing, readers and reading. We are constantly on the lookout for new ways of doing this. Andrew Motion, Chairman of our Literature Advisory Panel, has recently written to the Secretary of State about the loss to this country of writers' manuscripts and archives. These are sources of income for authors who are naturally going to seek the best price. In the current climate, that means abroad. Should readers from this country have to travel abroad to see the manuscripts and archives of English writers? Does the government think so little of the nation's literary culture that it is prepared to let such material vanish from these shores?

T. S. Eliot Prize-winner Don Paterson gently berates the Arts Council for undue emphasis on 'insane cross-disciplinary collaborations'. He reckons 'it's still easier to get money for that hypertext-poetry-with-throat-singing-and-freeform-macramé project than for anything sensible.' Not a thing wrong with a bit of throat-singing, I say, but I do know what he means. We need to fund writers to write. No gimmicks. No hoops to jump through beyond what is absolutely essential for the dictates of accountability. Direct support for the craft itself. As I have said, we do this through our annual Writers Awards scheme. We need to do more.

It is all very well to talk about commitment but what are the hard practicalities of addressing the cost of writing? What practical steps can the Arts Council take to help writers? What is the Arts Council's role in the support of the individual author?

Remember that we will continue to support a range of Literature organisations which are dedicated to the promotion of reading and writing. We will continue to develop initiatives in the world of education, libraries and broadcasting which encourage access to writers, writing and reading. The Arts Council is, after all, about making the arts available to as many people as possible.

None of this is possible without the writer. I would love to be able to say that, yes, we will take up Adrian Mitchell's idea of The Six Hundred, twenty thousand pounds per year for five years to two hundred novelists, two hundred poets and two hundred playwrights.

Something like that is not going to happen in an instant. What I can say is that the Arts Council is committed to devising new methods of support for writers. We are out there seeking new money, exploring new methods, advocating change. We have helped fund this publication. We want to encourage the debate, stimulate the opinion formers, put writers and writing at the heart of the cultural agenda. To achieve this we need the support of writers and readers, we need the support of the entire Literature constituency. We need to change attitudes.

The alternative is more of the same. Young writers struggling under financial pressure, older writers faced with hardship, the perennial diversion from the craft of writing. Surely Literature deserves better. Let us work together to eliminate the need for the 'beautiful begging letters'.

Gary McKeone
Literature Director, Arts Council of England

Acknowledgements

The publishers gratefully acknowledge permission to reprint the following work still in copyright:

The Cost of Letters by John Betjeman, © John Betjeman 1946, by permission of Desmond Elliott, Administrator of the Estate of Sir John Betjeman; The Cost of Letters by Elizabeth Bowen, © Elizabeth Bowen 1946, by permission of Curtis Brown Ltd., London; The Cost of Letters by Alex Comfort, © Alex Comfort 1946; The Cost of Letters (plus questions) by Cyril Connolly, © Cyril Connolly 1946, by permission of Rogers, Coleridge and White; The Cost of Letters by C. Day Lewis, © C. Day Lewis 1946, by permission of Peters Fraser & Dunlop Group Ltd; The Cost of Letters by Robert Graves, © Robert Graves 1946, by permission of Carcanet Press Ltd; The Cost of Letters by Robert Kee, © Robert Kee 1946; The Cost of Letters by Laurie Lee, © Laurie Lee 1946 by permission of Peters Fraser & Dunlop Group Ltd; The Cost of Letters by Rose Macauley, © Rose Macauley 1946, by permission of Peters Fraser & Dunlop; The Cost of Letters by George Orwell, © George Orwell 1946, by permission of Mark Hamilton, Literary Executor of the Estate of the late Sonia Brownell Orwell, and A. M. Heath & Co. Ltd.; The Cost of Letters by V. S. Pritchett, © V. S. Pritchett 1946, by permission of Peters Fraser & Dunlop Group Ltd; The Cost of Letters by Herbert Read, © Herbert Read 1946, by permission of David Higham Associates; The Cost of Letters by Stephen Spender, © Stephen Spender 1946, by permission of Lady Natasha Spender; The Cost of Letters by Dylan Thomas, © Dylan Thomas, by permission of David Higham Associates.

ACKNOWLEDGEMENTS